tell
me
more

tell me more

Building Trusted Client Relationships through Everyday Interactions

Deb Feder

GRAMMAR
FACTORY
— EST. 2013 —

Published by Grammar Factory Publishing.
25 Telegram Mews, 39th Floor, Suite 3906
Toronto, Ontario, Canada M5V 3Z1
www.grammarfactory.com

Feder, Deb
Tell Me More: Building Trusted Client Relationships through Everyday Interactions / Deb Feder.

Paperback ISBN 978-1-998756-78-0
Hardcover ISBN 978-1-998756-80-3
eBook ISBN 978-1-998756-79-7
Audiobook ISBN 978-1-998756-81-0

1. LAW056000 LAW / Law Office Management. 2. BUS020000 BUSINESS & ECONOMICS / Development / Business Development. 3. BUS058000 BUSINESS & ECONOMICS / Sales & Selling / General

Production Credits
Cover design by Designerbility
Book production and editorial services by Grammar Factory Publishing

*Because of her belief in potential and possibilities,
this book is my mother's legacy.*

*She taught me, by example, that our world is better
when we sit down, have a cup of coffee,
and learn about each other.*

Contents

In Preparation

On a cold, rainy night in Washington, D.C., I sat across the dinner table from a client engrossed in conversation while diving into our bowls of pasta. This was a casual dinner, and our conversation flowed naturally from college decisions to dogs, from law practice growth to LinkedIn, all without any one topic dominating. The talk flowed freely, and our chatter waned only when we noticed the time. We had no agenda; the focus was on reconnecting. Not because either of us "had to be there," but rather because we cared about each other and were interested in each other's success; the meal was bound to be at least enjoyable, perhaps even informative. It was all that and more.

There was an overarching pattern to each topic we discussed that night: the other party wanted to know more. And so, the conversation expanded. There was no forced effort to jump in and solve problems on the spot, but instead to find out more—to learn.

At their core, client relationships, including new business development efforts, are about building connections through dialogue with others. Through this exchange, it is possible to learn about clients, their ideas and challenges—both near- and long-term—and allow this knowledge to inform how you can be appropriately supportive.

This, in fact, is the role of the trusted thinking partner.

Done well, a conversation with a trusted thinking partner doesn't feel like an interrogation, interview, or pitch. It can be a simple discussion, a quick email, or a conversation had in passing. It could also be a longer strategy session or holding space for more complex problem-solving. Whatever form that conversation takes, it includes sharing lighter moments, knowing that someone else cares enough to remember you, and not thinking twice about revealing heavier thoughts that keep you up at night.

In our ever-busy world, responsiveness looks like the prize. But being a trusted thinking partner means being able to expand conversations. It's about being able to remain in conversations (even the difficult ones) and extend them in ways that would be impossible if you weren't truly present in the relationship. Staying present in the conversation starts by leaning into the opportunities waiting for you by adopting the practice of asking clients: *Tell Me More.*

Tell Me More is the strategy to lean on when you need support in a conversation. It puts the focus on your client and not you. It deepens your relationships with your colleagues, clients, and community.

When you are in a discussion with a client or colleague and not quite sure what they're looking for, ask them to *Tell You More.* This invites them to keep talking through the details so they can better explain their goals.

As the client, when you want your advisor to help you see the forest through the trees, but all you're hearing is a muddled mess, simply say *Tell Me More*. This allows you both to keep processing options until you come to the right solution that meets your needs.

When your mind starts to wander away during a conversation, and you lose track of what the other party is saying, pause and ask them to *Tell You More*. This acts as a trigger for your brain to refocus on the details needed to offer a thoughtful response.

In my first book, *After Hello: How to Build a Book of Business, One Conversation at a Time*, I describe how to set up your network of clients and how important it is to have the courage to truly step into conversations. This book is about what happens after you say *Hello*. It's about the opportunities you unlock when you build on those conversations by creating and nurturing client relationships. It's about opening dialogue, deepening relationships, and expanding your book of business through everyday interactions that focus on your clients. In a world filled with voices loudly proclaiming their expertise, *Tell Me More* is the subtle, sophisticated, yet simple strategy that lets you not only manage client relationships but also enrich and expand them through genuine curiosity about the other person.

While *Tell Me More* is just one example of the strategies this book lays out, it exemplifies the methodology of infusing your everyday interactions with simple steps to learn about your prospective and current clients, and their needs. The goal is to build and deepen trusted relationships and is the very reason why *Tell Me More* is the perfect title for this book.

The Client Relationship Journey

The initial goal of business development is to get you in the door and land the client. Then the focus shifts to providing outstanding advice so you're the one the client calls when they need expertise and experience and the one they refer to others who are seeking counsel. You'll eventually start to notice the signature components of a strong, healthy client relationship—the kind in which the attorney shows up and engages in the role of trusted thinking partner. Now, you are invested in the client's success and best interests, even when you've not been called upon for a specific task or activity. Reaching this stage depends on your approach, mindset and overall attitude toward your book of business.

The Mindset of the Trusted Thinking Partner

The right mindset starts with choosing to say *Hello*, being present for the conversation, and having the confidence to follow through on what comes next. It's believing in the power of the smallest interactions and showing up for the opportunities to grow your relationships with existing clients and bring new ones through your door. By being attentive in these moments, you prove to clients that *you* are the advisor they want and need in their corner.

Betting your practice on keeping just one or two long-standing clients happy and forgoing business development is risky. Consider the law firm of 30 years ago. Anchor institutions led the client roster, and there was little fear they would shop around for new counsel. Today, by contrast, rosters at law firms seem to change constantly. Lateral moves, retirements, in-house shifts, and more put the cadre of trusted advisors into near-constant flux. And when advisors change, a firm's relationship with its individual clients feels more tenuous. Ignoring relationships and the conversations your clients want to have leaves a gap for someone else to fill. This makes the quality of individual client relationships all the more important. Instead of clinging for dear life to the relationship for fear of it slipping away, the trusted thinking partner focuses on the whole relationship and acts as the support system their clients are seeking.

Who Can I Trust?

The role of in-house counsel has also changed. It now involves a careful blend of engaging in corporate strategy, managing legal initiatives, balancing budgets, implementing technology, and staying on top of institutional priorities. And all this has to be juggled while clients are seeking advisors who are the right fit for the needs of their legal and business teams. Finding outside advisors who fit this bill hinges on the question: *Who can I trust?*

The answer to that question cannot be found in a textbook or on the internet. And it is certainly not found in any self-assured handshake that accompanies the declaration, "You can trust me." It's answered through conversations, through the quality of work produced, through an inherent willingness to be present and focused on the client's particular goals and challenges. Experience and expertise are the essential foundation upon which trust begins, but once you know someone can do the work and do it well, trust takes on a deeper meaning, begging more profound questions:

- *Who will invest in understanding my problems?*
- *Who will learn more about me?*
- *Who will not let me down?*

Trust is not a one-way street but rather the overarching goal that you, your team, and your clients all seek. You hope that trust is established once a client signs that engagement letter or you turn in a solid first project. But it's what comes next that puts trust to the test.

That is what this book is about: keeping that trust and building on it, growing relationships and understanding how to deepen them, thus becoming your client's trusted thinking partner. *Tell Me More* is one important tool in doing so and an important reminder to always be present.

What Is a Trusted Thinking Partner?

Far too often, the client-lawyer relationship is thought of as piecework. First, the client reaches out for advice on a particular project or case and hires you to represent them. This is cause for great celebration and you realize there's an opportunity to build a book of business.

From there, you hope the client will entrust more work to you or ask you to provide a deeper level of expertise. When they do, your role becomes more that of the advisor who provides expertise when required. But beyond piecework, being a *thinking partner* to your client takes the relationship a significant step further—to the point where the connection is so deep that you think about your clients and their challenges even when you're not on the clock.

That might sound like a big ask, but think about it this way: if you confine your work with clients to a purely transactional level, then you will have to continually bid for their business. You may be an excellent attorney with an incredible team, but there is always someone else who is just as good, ready, willing, and able to provide that same level of service.

In choosing to be your client's trusted thinking partner and their constant collaborator in both the smallest moments and the biggest conversations, you forge a relationship well beyond the transactional level. You are not hired by someone to simply take a task off their plate but to partner with them through their future troubles and triumphs.

Think about this from the client's perspective. When you find an advisor who cares about the challenges you're facing as much as you do and who always shows up when you need them (or before you even realize you need them), budgets are no longer the only criteria for finding counsel. Your thinking partner is an advisor who will never let you down and will marshal their resources to make sure you have the other strategists and experts you need on your team. Your thinking partner and their team are the ones who help you navigate the complex questions that land on your desk all day, every day. They aren't only providing their expertise— they're also giving you the comfort and security that comes with implicit trust.

This "in it together" mentality is the cornerstone of client relationships that go deeper and last longer than any one project. A solid book of business is built through honest, curious conversations and interactions that move your client relationship toward a thinking partnership.

Once you decide the foundation of all your client relationships will include caring about the people involved, you never have to sell to them. If you do have to pitch for work against competitors, your reputation for being respectful, attentive, and authentic will precede you. Of course, you'll still need to answer the phone, help out when needed, and nurture your relationships, but all this will be so much easier because you are showing up as *you*.

Becoming a thinking partner also helps you better understand the person on the other side of the table or on the other end of the phone. You know why that one client is screaming, silent, or picking a fight for what seems like no reason. You recognize their stress responses and know which behaviors indicate genuine worry and anxiety, and which are negotiating tactics. You know how to distinguish between urgent matters of the highest priority and emotional pressures that are bubbling up to the surface. And the opposite is also true.

Your client will also better understand you, your practice, and your life. They'll respect your boundaries; you won't have to insist upon them. Your relationship will not be just about billable hours but rather a mutually beneficial working partnership in which you are each fully invested in the other's success. You want your client to shine, and they shine that light right back on you.

It's About Having the Right Tools

Clients' business priorities, legal priorities and the client team itself shift constantly. And so, the thinking partnership must evolve, too. The tools in this book are here to help you navigate those moments, starting with what happens *After Hello*. Throughout these chapters, you will find simple exercises to help you apply the ideas for you and with your clients. You can also access templates and resources that need a bit more space from an online Toolbox, which you can download here: https://debfeder.com/toolbox. You'll find these resources easy to test out, making them comfortable and energizing for you to use.

With that, let's try the first exercise to get you thinking about trusted relationships and how they show up for you.

Activity

Pick three advisors you have trusted over the years, and for each:

1. List at least three reasons you trusted them.

2. Next, describe the things they did to earn your trust.

3. Finally, note how your levels of trust or reliance on this person changed over time.

After you do this for each advisor, circle what they have in common.

The similarities you've identified in this exercise tell a story of how you build trust, how you pick those whom you rely on, and how you expand relationships. While each of your lists may look different, pay attention to what helped you trust each person you selected and how you were able to build this mutual trusting relationship.

This book will show you how to infuse these themes through-out your everyday interactions with clients as you learn to use strategic curiosity, pay attention to the perspective and details of others, and build trust by respecting the relationship. When you do this, mistakes will be forgiven, your work will be more fun and rewarding, and there will be more work in the future. By contrast, if you choose not to walk this path, you will embark on each project with uncertainty about the prospect of the next and never know where you stand with your clients.

The pages ahead will teach you not only to rethink how you bring in business but also how you approach the entire client relationship. You will discover how you can grow your practice further by implementing a truly client-centric approach using simple but wickedly effective strategies—strategies that are equally applicable to you and your clients because trust goes both ways. Together, we'll work through the process that takes you from that first *Hello* to *Tell Me More* and becoming the trusted thinking partner that clients want and need.

Part One

**Everyday Habits
that Build Dynamic
Client Relationships**

Get Organized Enough

A thinking partner invests in the small moments, so the big projects launch with ease.

Ten years ago, I facilitated a retreat that forever changed the work that I do. It was an intense two days in a room full of highly accomplished, professional women. The walls were covered with hand-written affirmations and commitments to big goals. These ranged from exponentially growing their book of business to running for office and more. The time spent in that room was impactful, and everyone walked away with a unique action plan of their own.

At the end of the retreat, I asked one final, simple question: "What will you do tomorrow to move your goal forward?"

The replies stunned me. After marveling about the incredible breakthroughs they'd had over the past few days, each person answered with some version of: "As soon as I get organized, I'll be ready to jump in."

That these accomplished lawyers, business owners, and civic leaders needed to "get organized" before leaning into their highest goals left me feeling confused and even slightly defeated. Yet, when I paused and considered these responses more deeply, it became clear that the chaos of their everyday work was getting in the way of their greater goals and distorting their priorities.

Before they began, they wanted to feel organized.

Note that I did not say to *be* organized. After much inquiry and conversations, what became apparent was this was a quest to feel organized. Seeking the *feeling* of being organized— is a desire to be in control and understand what is important for you to tackle next (whether for your substantive work or business development efforts). When you feel organized, it allows you to be responsive to client needs, not reactive. It lets you shift from simply diving into the most urgent needs as they arise to having the time and space to be truly present for client conversations and check-ins. This builds trust and, often, creates possibilities for the next project or idea.

After hearing all these ambitious and successful women effectively "kick the can down the road" on their goals, I knew that building a book, nurturing client relationships, and overseeing a law practice required a solid system of resources and tools that provide the space to deal with the everyday intensity. The goal is to develop a system that gets you organized *enough* to efficiently manage your days, know what needs to be done and by when, and deliver your work with excellence.

Step one to getting organized enough is simply to get a clear idea of what a good system looks like and how it can support the growth of your practice. In searching for such a system, you'll likely encounter a barrage of productivity apps designed to help manage your tasks, your calendar, and your brainstorms, all of which will beg for your attention (and money).[1] You name it, and there's a product claiming to save you hours of work by streamlining tasks. I'm all about a great tool, but to make any tool worth even the smallest monthly fee, you have to use it, and it must work with and for both you and your goals. My suggestion? Before trying to implement anything, let's get rid of the tools you have now that you're not using.

Activity

Before adding new solutions to your toolbox, let's get rid of what you don't need, starting with all the apps loaded on your phone. Think of it like your closet: if you haven't used an app in the last year, ask yourself if it's truly necessary. If it's not, delete it. While you're at it, list out all the subscriptions you're paying for. Are there any you're not using? If so, now is a good time to cancel them.

Step two in the journey to feeling organized is not digital but analog: tidying your workspace. The busier you get, the more reminders and ideas get logged on sticky notes and scribbled in the margins of printed documents. So, take ten minutes, throw on some music, and start cleaning. As you find notes, transcribe the information to a single list on a sheet of paper. This allows you to see all there is to do in one spot.

---

1   According to Grand View Research, the productivity app market was a $53.1 billion industry in 2022 and is expected to grow at a compound annual rate of 14% through 2030. That's a lot of options! Learn more about this in their article: https://www.grand-viewresearch.com/industry-analysis/productivity-management-software-market

A good cleaning party is satisfying. Seeing your desk free of clutter and your floor cleared of stacks of paper, files, and notebooks creates a sense of calm and joy. It's the feeling you yearn for while working on big projects or cases that don't allow the time for lunch breaks, let alone filing your papers.

Now that you've decluttered your digital space and your working space, you should already be feeling more organized. The next step is to organize your professional network. This will help you develop clients who lay the foundation for your practice and help it grow and prosper. You need to recognize who you know. Doing so helps you to track your conversations and connections, which provides the tools to tackle many of the recommendations in this book. For this, I have a simple solution.

Build Your Rolodex

When I was little, my dad's family owned and managed apartment buildings in Cedar Rapids, Iowa. My Grandma Ruth, who owned the company with her sons, often took me to work with her as she spent the day managing one of the complexes. Grandma Ruth would allow me the privilege of using her ginormous desktop adding machine, in which I always found great joy. Also sitting on that desk was the most important thing in the office: her Rolodex. It was bursting at the seams with hundreds and hundreds of tiny cards representing every person she had ever met.

Each card in that Rolodex was meticulously filled out with the name of the person, how Ruth had met them, any particularities about them she thought were important, and, of course, up-to-date contact information. I might have added my own card to that file a few times, with diligent notes about my area of expertise and the things I loved. Ruth's notes about her connections were always precise, so I wanted to make sure she had it down that I preferred chocolate cream pie and her tuna sandwiches. (A girl like me could not be too careful about making sure she got what she wanted.)

There are so many lessons I've taken from Ruth. She understood that a relationship was not merely about collecting names and phone numbers (and now, email addresses and myriad social media handles). A good networking tool tells you far more about the person behind the information.

With so much in our lives now automated, we've lost much of that personal information about each other that Ruth diligently noted and kept updated. Over time, the Rolodex became a physical address book for many of us, and we held tight to it for as long as possible. But today, we've come to rely almost exclusively on the contacts feature of our email systems, more complex relationship management systems, and social media platforms. All of these provide the illusion that we're well organized and well connected.[2]

However, without a more defined approach to keep track of conversations (and your business development efforts), you will spend too much time trying to figure out who you need to contact, how to find them, and trying to recall what you need to discuss with them. This makes following up on opportunities

---

2   One organizational tool for networking is a customer relationship management system (or CRM) that captures every touchpoint with contacts in your network. These tools have been used by sales teams to nurture relationships and track the sales cycle, with some progress made in creating such systems for the legal industry. The goal of this chapter is not to clean up all of your contacts, nor populate a CRM with each relationship. A good CRM works with the strategies mentioned here, but still requires a current nurturing list that we are about to set up.

unnecessarily complex and stands directly in the way of building good client relationships. It also flies in the face of feeling organized enough to nurture these relationships.

Remember, the goal here is to gather your connections and contacts in a way that makes it easiest to have conversations—*real* conversations where you can be curious and learn from and about your clients, especially when they are Ideals[3] (a term I use in *After Hello* that describes the ideal client) or those working with them. Because the more you know about them, the stickier your connections become.

Without getting too techy, you need to have a place you trust where you can keep the information you need. While the exact method doesn't matter, it should be a system that you will actually use.

There are many excellent apps and tools available to keep track of your network. While there isn't space in this book to list them all, and many of them may become quickly outdated, there is a question you need to ask yourself, regardless of the tool you use. That is:

> *What does it mean to be organized enough to know your network, nurture your connections, track your conversations and opportunities with them, and follow up and follow through on your obligations?*

The answer? You need to be organized enough to maintain the consistent momentum that helps to maximize the efforts that turn those conversations into incredible opportunities. You guessed it: I have a plan for this.

---

3   Ideals are those "perfect" clients that magically align with your focus, your approach, your rates, and your boundaries (not to be confused with Targets which we talk about later).

I'd like to introduce your Networking Nurture List.[4] Your Networking Nurture List is not your entire contact list, and it doesn't require you to go back and fill in everyone you have ever met. But, it *does* require that you start today and track your conversations and networking efforts going forward so you can follow through on your next steps without struggling to remember your plans when you finally find the time to focus on business development.[5]

Activity

It's now time to modernize the Rolodex and create your Networking Nurture List. Again, this will not be a list of everyone you know, just those you are actively nurturing or in contact with right now. It will evolve and change over time. To begin, open a spreadsheet and set up columns for the following:

1. First and last name (two columns)
2. Company (or how you know the person)
3. Date of last connection
4. Notes

As you initiate conversations with more people, add them to the list. As you continue to use your Nurture List and grow your relationships, it will grow as well.

---

4   This will be often referred to as your Nurture List (or List) throughout the book. Whatever you call it, it's that list where you keep track of who you are actively engaged with (or want to be) for networking and business development purposes.

5   We use this list frequently in our weekly Focus30 networking session. Knowing who you want and need to connect with and tracking what happens with those efforts helps you recognize (and celebrate) all you are doing to nurture and grow your network and the business development results that happen with this effort.

The next step in building your Nurture List is to expand it by adding the people you know and the people you want to know better, all focused on deepening your network and business development goals.

Remember Who You Know

Getting organized enough with your networking efforts starts with brainstorming. The goal is to make a few lists to simply prove (to yourself) that you do, in fact, know quite a few people. It is also a time to recognize that your "work" and "life" intertwine more than you realize and lean into all those relationships to enrich and expand your view of your practice, supporting clients and, ultimately, bringing in business.

Consider the following four categories of people within your network, and pick two or three people from each one to add to your Nurture List (you can, of course, add more later):

1. **The Speed Dials**: The people you know really well. You would have them over for Sunday brunch, and popping into each other's texts is completely normal. They may be both your SOS call and your celebration buddy.

2. **The Everydays**: The people you work with and interact with frequently. They might be current clients, colleagues or possibly the neighbor you see all the time. You know them well and want to nurture the relationship, but they aren't quite your BFF. Sometimes, you can pivot these more casual relationships into a business relationship once you've figured out a strategy to make it happen.

3. **The Connected-ish**: The people you *kind of* know. You may call to ask them a question but would not send them a wedding or baby gift. You see them in the carpool line, wave to them at a networking event, and often have common friends and colleagues.

4. **The Don't Know Well Yet (or Anymore)**: The people you remember but don't know very well. They could be in your practice group, but you've never spoken to them. Or they work with your clients, and your paths constantly cross, but you've never paused to say more than *Hello*. They could also be people you knew "way back when" and who, for all intents and purposes, you'd need to reintroduce yourself to. (More on these lost connections below.)

Another reminder: this is not an exercise to list *everyone* you know. If you're struggling to start, just begin by adding people you're actively working and engaging with. And if you can't think of anyone to add from a category yet, be patient. It might feel weird at first, but if you start with your office colleagues, the names of clients whose emails are sitting in your inbox, and connections you haven't talked to in forever, the names will start to flow.

One quick note for putting these lists together: Too often, my clients overthink who to include on their Nurture List. There is an instinct to leave people off the list, and your brain tries to give you reasons not to include someone. Those reasons include:

- They already have counsel.

- They won't remember you.

- Someone else at the firm owns the bigger relationship, so you don't know if you're allowed to talk to them.

- There is only one chance to reach out to them.

- They're too busy.

- They mentioned how much they hate email, so it's better to see what happens when you run into them.

- They'll think it's weird of you to reach out.

The list could go on and on. Many of these reasons are valid, but they don't necessarily need to be stumbling blocks in your networking plan, so include the individuals anyway. Remember, you're just making a list. The goal isn't to pitch your services to all of these people; you simply need to know who you know.

Activity

Let's give your Nurture List a boost. A great place to start is with your current colleagues since internal networking is just as important as external networking. Law is a profession in constant motion, so there is always someone within your organization or firm who you should reconnect with, meet, or learn more about. These are your internal clients and collaboration partners. This category includes summer associates (they will be in leadership roles before you retire, or at least working on your teams), as well as the lateral hires who are expanding your team.

Think about the colleagues at your firm and those you collaborate with often, and add the following to your List:

- two people you work with all the time (Everydays),

- two people in other offices you would like to work with again (Connected-ish), and

- two new people who joined your practice group (Don't Know Well Yet).

Starting with these, you'll discover that you really *do* know a lot of people. It may come as a shock to you, but while you've been head down, working, you've been gathering connections right and left without even knowing it.

The Social Depth of Your Network

Your Nurture List is starting to take shape, but let's now consider your online networks. The rise of social media has resulted in many disparate lists of contacts across many different platforms. This can easily feel unruly and expansive. To rein these lists in, you need to include relevant contacts from those networks you hope to nurture on your Nurture List.

While I would suggest starting with LinkedIn, due to its popularity as a professional networking platform, each of your social media accounts is filled with people who would be great additions to your List.[6] While many people you are connected to on LinkedIn and other networks may not be a part of your inner circle, they most certainly could be a Connected-ish. A quick click into their profile can give you more information about why you might connect with them and what they're up to now.

It's also worth considering the incredible networks you've built in online groups (where the law moms and dads, fitness enthusiasts, and virtual book clubs are hanging out and sharing ideas, just to name a few). These are people you know and often interact with (often as Everydays), so scroll through your network and pay attention to who you know. You may see some of the names you thought of in the first brainstorm, which often happens and is a hint that the relationship might be a bit more advanced than you had thought. You will also notice names from past deals, school connections, and former jobs. Let's add them to the list.

Don't Forget the Lost Connections

An incredible amount of business development can happen through rekindling conversations with classmates, clients, colleagues, and people in the community who used to be an integral part of your life until your lives moved in different directions. Said another way: you knew each other well "back then," and you would appreciate (if not *love*) finding out what they're up to and explore new conversations and

---

6 Now is a good time to get social. I am most active on LinkedIn (https://linkedin.com/in/bizdeb), and post videos from time to time on YouTube (https://www.youtube.com/@bizdeb). While I have Facebook and Instagram accounts, my presence there can be described as spotty. Find me, hit connect, and send me a message to let me know where to find you.

opportunities with these lost, but not forgotten, connections. Here are a few ways to jog your memory of people you have known along the way:

Classmates

One type of connection that is often forgotten is your former classmates. Do your best to recall who you knew from study groups and late-night cram sessions. Those trench battles create such a strong bond that no matter how much time has passed, you can pick right up and remember all the jokes (and all the pizza) that you shared.

LinkedIn is your friend for discovering where they are now. Some have gone into law-adjacent positions (like legal tech), while others have gone in-house, and there might be potential for them to become clients when you reach out and reconnect. Some will have stayed in private practice, and because they already know you, they could be incredible referral partners.

Former partners and bosses

Another group you may have forgotten to keep in touch with are the first partners and bosses you worked with. These are people who invested a tremendous amount in your success: dragging you to meetings, pointing out your sloppy mistakes, and giving you second (and third) chances because they had "been there themselves." You learned about their lives and their families while traveling to see clients and became a better lawyer by working for them. You need to reach back out to them because they're interested in how you turned out, and your shared history makes it easy to jump back into conversations. If nothing else, remember to thank them for their support in launching your career.

Former clients

Think of the clients you worked with in the early days of your practice; how they joked with you through the misery of the case before trial and the long hours trying to get that deal closed on New Year's. They know you, and you know them. You know what they order at a restaurant or what they snack on when they're stressed. You may have lost touch after they moved to another company or into another role because these connections often advanced in their career just like you did. And, just like you, they will likely be excited to reconnect, reminisce, and catch up.

Keep brainstorming. Consider who else might be a good connection today and open up the next conversation (or even opportunity) for the future. Now, look at your List and realize this very important fact:

You. Know. People.

That is all that matters today.

Holding Out for the Target

One of the categories you might notice is missing from the strategy so far is the target client (or Target, as I call them). This is the client who seems like an amazing catch and lines up perfectly with the work you do. They are the career-changing opportunity that you obsessively overthink while ignoring the rest of your networking opportunities. But when you focus intensely on a Target, you not only miss out on the possibility of forging a real relationship with them but also on the other conversations happening around you. On the other hand, sometimes you hold out way too long to make the first move as you wait for a clear and unambiguous sign that the Target is ready to engage with you. The reality is that a great book of business can be generated without ever needing to throw all that energy into chasing a Target.

Keep It Up

Now that you've started and expanded your Rolodex (aka Networking Nurture List), you're ready to use this information in a way that works for you and your practice. You're going to get to know your community in a whole new way, allowing the great clients you are meant to work with to fall right into your lap. The Toolbox has a networking checklist to give this process some momentum and help you maintain this new focus on nurturing your connections.[7]

As you advance, keep your Nurture List updated with the conversations, requests, and relationships you're building; this will become increasingly important. It is the simplest way to stay organized enough to spot the next opportunity and allow your client relationships to flourish.

---

7   Check out the networking checklist in the Toolbox, or send me a note and request a guest pass to Focus30, where we put this into action each week (hello@debfeder.com).

Choose Your Words Wisely

Clients remember how you make them feel with the words you choose to use.

While I have a lot to say about modern education, there is nothing I learned to dread more than quizzing my kids on vocabulary. This started in the fourth grade and has not stopped. Weekly lists of words I have never used, cannot pronounce, and have assured my children no one really uses— words like "mellifluous," "philippic," and "contumacious." How would you react at a concert if your friend looked at you and yelled to you how "mellifluous" the singer was? Would it not suffice to say she's "really good"?

This kind of superfluous language is all too common when trying to sound impressive, like when awkward jargon gets thrown around in conversations, creating a wall between advisor and client. It's often simply a result of being nervous and wanting to sound smart, yet it blocks true connection. To bring in business and develop deeper client relationships, you need to bridge this divide. When you understand your client's level of knowledge and facility with the subject matter and legal framework, you can tailor your words and approach appropriately at every step.

You don't have to sound mundane or overly colloquial. Indeed, there can be great value in commanding an expansive and robust vocabulary. But your choice of words matters. As with anything, the devil is in the details. For example, you know that a well-crafted email has a better chance of landing than a sloppy one, but did you know that research shows that starting an email with a more informal greeting ("Hi," "Hello," or even "Hey") is more likely to garner a response?[8] And emails ending in "Thanks" tend to get a higher reply rate?[9]

Lawyers spend years learning to decipher the law and master written and verbal advocacy but often struggle to compose a three-sentence email inviting a client to lunch. Your words need to resonate with their reader (whether a client, an adversarial party, another colleague, or the rest of the team supporting the project).

Our everyday word choices are often instinctive, but when planning deliberate communication, there are a few basics that will help you choose words that connect with clients, convey your intent, and get your conversation across the finish line.[10]

---

8   In case you want to geek out on the email research with me, check out this research and analysis for email openings and response rates by Brendan Greenley, "How to Start an Email: An Email Openings Analysis of 300,000+ Messages." You can find the article here: https://qz.com/work/1184551/how-to-start-an-email-an-email-openings-analysis-of-300000-messages

9   The research looked at three variants of the closing "Thanks," and overall, they had a 62% response rate, compared to others such as "Best regards," which was just under a 53% response rate. More on this in the article: https://blog.boomerangapp.com/2017/01/how-to-end-an-email-email-sign-offs/

10   I do love to nerd out on the language and choices that distinguish between an "okay" email and a great one. A great exercise for crafting one of your most important email templates is knowing what you want to talk about. The Toolbox has a great template to get you started brainstorming and putting your first email together. Remember to download it at https://debfeder.com/toolbox.

Notice the Words Around You

The simplest strategy for choosing the right words and tone is to pay closer attention to everyday conversations you're already involved in and near to. The goal here is not to copy anyone but rather to step outside the discussion and notice how others engage in conversations. Some will be models to emulate, and others will make you shudder; most will land somewhere in between and provide anchors for you to strike your right balance.

Before we develop your approach, let's consider a few extreme examples:

- **The Cringe-y Conversationalist**. Typically full of puffery and braggadocio, this archetype forces everyone to listen to self-serving accolades and tedious details of their (supposedly) exotic (and quite possibly boring) fishing trip, even in an email intended to organize a meeting for next Tuesday.

- **The Super-Smoothster**. This type of conversationalist is dripping with compliments and falls all over themselves trying to win the favor of colleagues and clients. After a while, it may get as cringe-y as the type above, yet somehow, it often feels necessary to copy if it seems to be working (hint: it usually isn't).

- **The Scholar**. This person knows their stuff and loves to talk about it, going into the minute details usually reserved for Wikipedia or a law journal article. They're interesting at first, but as the conversation drags on, a pattern of dry facts often develops. Beware of yawns.

- **The Magician**. This type of person connects everyone while weaving in their expertise in a subtle and sophisticated way. They can start with a mundane topic like peanut butter and jelly sandwiches and then (somehow) organically progress to more important business matters. Pure magic.

Can you guess which approach I'd choose? The Magician is a blend of connecting others, sharing expertise, and resonating with clients. It is one that can be woven seamlessly into your work, and most naturally builds into your everyday interactions. To develop your own approach to becoming a Magician, there are a few rules that will help to get your point across.

Your Conversation Rule Book

Let's look at a few simple rules for choosing the words you use in your conversations. A sophisticated conversation strategy blends the art of *what to say* with *how to make it resonate*. And it can help you with even the most functional emails, giving you the opportunity to grow your role as a thinking partner.

Rule 1: Be Polite

It turns out that all those reminders you were given growing up about how "gracious words go a long way" were spot on. Using "please" and "thank you" in conversations will help advance your mission. This does not mean you need to fall all over yourself with compliments; too many niceties feel insincere.[11] The most important point is to remember the long-lasting impact of good manners. When hurrying on to the next task, email, or conversation, it's easy to forget to

---

11 A good place to start is to make sure you use your client's name and spell it correctly before crafting the perfect email.

offer an intentional expression of gratitude.[12] Take that extra moment; it's worth it.

While a written (or even digital) thank you note is always impactful, polite words can also be sprinkled into each of your more casual, everyday interactions. Simple word choices go a long way, and here is a list of some of the more popular, polite terms and phrases:

1. Please
2. Thank you (thanks)
3. Much appreciated
4. I'm looking forward to...
5. I appreciate the chance to...
6. With gratitude...
7. You are most welcome

Create your own list of polite words—ones that sound authentically like you and that you know are noticed and appreciated by the people you work with each and every day.

Rule 2: Leave the Bad Words Behind

Full disclosure: I've been known to use some spicy language from time to time. I probably started learning that vocabulary when I boarded the school bus in kindergarten. Working on fast-paced deal teams with too little sleep and too much caffeine also "enhanced" my coarse language skills in tense moments, and for good reason. There is even

---

12 A gratitude and appreciation form email can be found in the Toolbox.

research showing that the use of profanity can reduce pain.[13] However, there is a time and place for curse words. They aren't for every situation, especially with someone you don't know that well. A strong word can create impact, but it loses its impact if it is overused or misplaced. So, the rule here is simple: watch your words and read the room carefully before using words that others might find inappropriate.

Clients hire a trusted thinking partner to represent them and show up in their stead. So, your initial conversations with clients should demonstrate the tone and tenor that they can expect from you when acting on their behalf, particularly in high-stakes situations. When you want to win that new client and make a solid first impression, remember that your word choices matter.

Recently, a colleague shared an anecdote about a top candidate's choice to curse in a job interview. It caused many in the room to raise their eyebrows, ask tougher questions, and ultimately decide it was too risky of a hire. Interviewers concluded that the candidate's lack of judgment was the opposite of what was needed in the role they were interviewing for. Overuse of four-letter words can be perceived as a sign of limited vocabulary. Even more simply, curse words can offend, which is certainly not your intent or the goal when it comes to client relationships.

I'm not going to give you an exercise to list out all the bad words you know. Instead, I want you to start thinking of words you can use to make a point with impact but without

---

13 If you want to dive into some of the research behind profanity and your brain, check out Emma Byrne's book *Swearing is Good for You: The Amazing Science of Bad Language*, 1st edition.

offending others. This exercise will remind you that your vocabulary can be reinvigorated by your word choice.

Rule 3: Be Specific

On a road trip, you need to know where you're going before you set out; it's the same with a conversation. When you consider where you want to take the conversation before you start typing or grab your phone, you can set the correct tone and tenor and avoid misunderstandings. For example, if you want to set up a lunch but say, "Let's connect soon," that vagueness will likely elicit an equally vague reply.

This rule is critical when handing out projects that you want teams to tackle with gusto. When details are vague, it's hard to meet expectations. Before you make a request or invitation, make a list of what you want so you can articulate it well. A clear request increases trust a great deal.

However, there is a fine line here. Being too specific can annoy people and may actually dissuade them from responding. I can't tell you how many times I've seen people send messages like this:

> *I am available on the 25th at 11:30 a.m. at the café, or on the 29th for a late lunch at 4 p.m. closer to the north of town. Please let me know which of these two options works for you.*

Instead of being helpful, this creates an obstacle if you can't make either option work. It's the lunch invitation version of a multiple-choice test, which can overwhelm the other person and create a new hurdle to overcome in your relationship-building plans.

A simple approach for invitations like this is to ask the client what works for their schedule in the next couple of weeks or offer two to three large windows of time when you can be available. This creates flexibility and removes the "now or never" energy from the interaction.

You can practice bringing specificity to conversations by listing all the things you want to say before you start writing. Then, scratch off anything that seems too aggressive or demanding. When you think you've caught them all, consider what you need to add back in to make sure you can still convey your thoughts and advance the conversation. You should now have a much tighter plan for your communication.

Rule 4: Pick Your Emotional Undertone

When you're a trusted thinking partner, you have the privilege of being in the room for high-stakes discussions when emotions might be running high. Your ability to stay calm in these high-energy situations is a powerful signal about your broader capabilities. Knowing how to speak from a place of calm confidence allows you to choose your words wisely. Here are some suggestions for how to do just that, in a variety of settings:

- Before you hit send on an email reply, take a couple of deep breaths and even step away for a moment.

- Before you walk into a networking room, take a couple of deep breaths.

- Before you respond to a client's invitation to a pitch, move past the anxious excitement by taking a couple of deep breaths.

- When in the middle of a heated discussion, don't try to match the decibel level in the room; instead, take two deep breaths.

You probably caught the pattern: Two deep breaths before taking action can help you assess the situation better, read the room, ask better questions, and carry the right conversation forward. Studies have found that focusing on your breath is directly connected to your stress response. It helps you stay calm through that adrenaline rush when you sense something good is about to happen or the anxiety when you think everything is falling apart.[14] When you're in a situation charged with high energy and high stakes, staying calm and thinking clearly will win the day.

Knowing how you want to be seen by your client—as the expert and advisor—is a powerful next step in creating an environment that fosters positive dialogue. I love helping lawyers learn to slow down their breathing, and how using this technique can affect the mood of a room. If you walk into the room with big energy, you'll attract the more gregarious people. If you walk in timidly, you're more difficult for others to connect with; your energy says, *Don't bother me*. Instead, take a couple of deep breaths, introduce yourself, and engage in the conversations happening around you. This creates the energy that lets you sense the mood of others and encourage them to connect with you.

---

14 Harvard Health Publishing's article, "Relaxation techniques: Breath control helps quell errant stress response," provides the background and practical steps to practice deep breathing techniques. For more information about this, visit the following article: https://www.health.harvard.edu/mind-and-mood/relaxation-techniques-breath-control-helps-quell-errant-stress-response

Rule 5: Consider Your Timing

Up to now, we've covered rules about what to say; this rule is about balancing efficiency (given the quantity of communication demanding your attention) with the effectiveness and impact of your message. To support this balance, it's important to keep your inbox tidy enough that you know what's in it: all those emails are potential opportunities. When you miss the "diamond in the rough" (or see it but fail to reply), you may lose the chance to be included or expand the work with a current client. Said another way, if you delay unreasonably, the client may shop around for someone else. Reasonableness is the rule here—I'm not suggesting you jump every time a client calls. Simply keep the client's communication preferences top of mind to allow you to effortlessly remain in the loop for their legal needs.

A blend of productivity strategy (managing the inbox) and conversation launchers (what to say to keep the door open and the discussion moving forward) is helpful here. First, you must manage your inbox and incorporate it into your conversation strategy; then, make sure client conversations are not met with silence.[15]

With a better sense of the conversations you need to engage in, timing cues can help build trust. For example:

1. If you forgot to reply to a message, own it with a quick apology. That helps keep the project and conversation on track so the client doesn't feel like you dropped the ball (or completely forgot about them).

---

15 Check out the email triage strategy in the Toolbox. This #BizDeb staple is often the game changer in getting your inbox to work with and for you and your big goals.

2. If you send a second message before the client has replied to the first one, make it clear that you don't want to nag them but simply want to make sure they received the information, especially if the content is time sensitive.

3. If a conversation has gone stale, reboot it with words like "it's been way too long," and jumpstart that reconnection.

While I spend a fair amount of time helping clients reengage with relationships that have gone dormant, or with a potential opportunity that feels lost, it is always easier to stay on top of what's current than work through the complicated path of refreshing a relationship that's gone cold.

Writing Your Conversation Rule Book

Try out each of the strategies and "rules" covered in this chapter, and then take some time to create your own rulebook with the goal of bringing in work and attracting Ideals to engage you and your firm.[16]

In addition to the five rules discussed in this chapter, remember—your language choices, in both written and verbal conversations, need to sound like you. Admiring how others communicate to clients or even copying one of my email templates is efficient, but it's critical that your communication sounds like *you*, not me or someone else. If you hire someone else to write for you, clients will be confused when they pick up the phone, and your tone and approach don't

---

16 Yup—the Toolbox has a template for writing your conversation rulebook too.

match how you write.[17] If you heavily proof formal emails but are incredibly casual in person, that, too, can cause confusion. For your expertise, your ideas, and your self to shine through in client conversations, your word choice, approach, and tone deserve thoughtful, proactive attention.

Your Everyday Words Build Trust

Consider what we've talked about so far: building a book of business begins with the desire to bring in a client. Deciding to show up authentically and allow clients to get to know you and your expertise creates the foundation for it. Building on this, you are engaged with clients and colleagues during your day-to-day work as well as across larger projects and opportunities. Each interaction can be a development opportunity. That means your words, level of responsiveness, and temperament matter. Too often, the focus is strictly on the big moments, yet it's the everyday small talk that leads the way to great relationships, and that's what we'll learn about next.

---

17 I would be remiss if I didn't mention the increasing tendency to rely on AI to create communications. For those with a sophisticated eye, like the sort of clients you're working with, a computer-generated message can be spotted a mile away. Why? Because AI doesn't have the correct judgment or knowledge of your clients and their intended big goals. It might be a good start when you are stuck, but then use your own judgment and knowledge to carry the conversation forward.

Small Talk is Really Big Talk

When you treat relationship-building and networking as an exercise in client acquisition, you will miss the opportunity standing right in front of you.

I distinctly remember jumping on a video call in 2020 with a publication editor from Spain. Upon learning that I live in Kansas City, he exclaimed: "Mahomes!" (as in Patrick, the KC Chiefs' star quarterback). This launched us into a discussion of his travels to the United States, his hopes to visit the Midwest, and the differences between Chicago and Kansas City (primarily the winter weather and lack of a lake). As our small talk progressed, he got a sense of me as a person and as a storyteller, which supported the purpose of our call: we were discussing the possibility of me contributing articles to his publication for international law firms. In turn, I was able to discern his attitude about work, the quality of the publication, and his balanced approach to work and life. All that came from a conversation that started with a single word: "Mahomes!"

This book was written in the lead up to and following the Chiefs' 2024 repeat Super Bowl win (and Taylor Swift's sudden interest in the team), when all eyes were on Kansas City.

People visiting the city were reading up on KC's famous barbecue and wanted to compare the local sauces to their own regional favorites. Clients who had been here for a retreat were sending me notes about must-visit restaurants they'd read about and the museum they wanted to visit. What many had considered a flyover spot is now on the radar for people around the world. It has evolved into genuine curiosity about my hometown—which, in turn, allows me to learn more about where others live.

Small talk grants access to deeper knowledge about your clients and colleagues, including their work history, priorities, and values. Through small talk, I've learned much more about the humans involved in my work without ever having to pull out an agenda and "get down to business." It has also made business discussions easier to initiate and far more effective because we started out with banter and moved forward from that foundation.

Small Talk Matters

Pause and think about what is actually involved in small talk. It's both a little bit of everything and not much at all. You joke with the clients about impromptu trips to catch a great dinner, new cities you have visited, and which museum you loved most in Paris. You talk about last night's game and laugh at old stories. Relationships are cemented in these moments of everyday connection. They are the conversations that stay mostly on the light side, and yet they can easily morph into a deeper discussion and strategy session when necessary.

These light conversations can happen at networking events, at the beginning of video conferences, in the elevator, or over email. They demonstrate how well you know someone, and by paying attention to small details, you can show your care for and knowledge of them as a human being, not just the source of billable hours. These are key ingredients to the trust-building recipe.

Finding openings for small talk can feel daunting, but it's a great way to connect with people. I've had clients call me from outside a networking event, cocktail party, or morning meeting because they were worried about walking in the door. The story is always the same:

> *I'm not sure what to say or who I will know, so what's the point of going? I look and sound awkward and never get anything out of these moments anyway.*

Yet once they get over that initial anxiety, the event is consistently a success. This happens not just because they walked into the room but because they walked in with a strategy.

The best way to make your entry into a small-talk moment less stressful is to dispense with the presumption that you'll walk out of it with any tangible outcome. A signed engagement letter or new project shouldn't be the goal because that isn't how it happens.

This might be the most important lesson in this book (and why it is the epigraph for the chapter):

> *When you treat relationship-building and networking as an exercise in client acquisition, you will miss the opportunity standing right in front of you.*

Not only can this self-serving focus on sales be spotted a mile away, but it also creates an awkward atmosphere in which everyone is holding their cards close to their chest. It makes people reluctant to open up, and opening up is critical to better, more authentic connections. Said another way: in the effort to get the client, you may just lose the connection.

Small Talk is Opportunity

Small-talk interactions are an incredible way to get to know a client's tone and demeanor. Are they more formal in their approach? What are they interested in when they're relaxed? Small talk on the phone often starts with the immediate context of the day: updates on families, teams, or what's bugging them. Paying attention provides awesome insight into your clients' work habits and life.

Small talk can also reflect someone's preferences and values, which allows you to gather and integrate these essential insights. Paying attention to details helps you make choices that work for your clients. If you continue to invite someone who abstains from alcohol to wine tastings, you might think they're blowing you off when they don't accept your invitations. Similarly, if a client is vegan and you gift them a Steak of the Month Club subscription for the holidays, you've not done them or yourself any favors. I have seen both these mistakes, and not only does the client usually give away the gifts, but there is also often a side comment to others about how the gesture missed the mark. This all might be avoided by paying closer attention to the small talk.

Small-talk conversations are trust-building, relationship-strengthening opportunities that are out in the open, waiting for you. Clients don't always want to talk about the case, deal, or strategy, and neither should you.

SMALL TALK IS REALLY BIG TALK

Research shows that a third of communication consists of small talk.[18] Chatter, banter, and chit-chat are often considered trivial but provide a strong foundation on which to build the next level of your trusted thinking partnership. They help navigate a relationship toward an end goal (such as a pitch) through the connections and rhythms created by the banter. Small talk creates the foundation of authentic human connection, allowing you to get in sync with other people and start developing a tighter bond over shared experiences and stories.

Putting small talk into action, you can start to open the window to see the next opportunities. While relationships often start with small talk and then progress to more meaningful conversation, this stage is circled back to over and over again in the life cycle of every relationship. You might as well get comfortable with it.

Building Rapport Through Casual Banter

Small talk can be about more than just the weather. Early-stage banter is a chance to get to know someone on different levels, so it can, and should, span a variety of topics. Great small talk takes advantage of the moment to scaffold the conversation and learn more about the work, goals, and ideas of a client without going all in on them quite yet.

Developing your own unique approach to small talk allows you to relax and enjoy the moment. This will help you walk

---

18 Want to dive into the science behind chit-chat with me? Check out: "The Secret Science Behind Small Talk," which you can find here: https://www.casbo.org/3-techniques-to-derail-procrastination-2/

into a room with more pep in your step and carry on a more meaningful conversation. What won't serve you well with small talk is slavishly copying the approach of others or jumping into that gregarious conversation at the cocktail party if that's not your style (if it is, then feel free to join the big group laughing by the bar). Pick a discussion topic that is comfortable for you, and you'll have a much easier time engaging in small talk.

Activity

Small talk starts by identifying certain buckets of conversation topics that work well for you. We will develop your banter strategy in a bit, but for now, let's focus on finding a few go-to topics that you're familiar with and comfortable talking about. Of course, they should be topics that others are likely to enjoy as well.

1. Start brainstorming with one simple question: *If you can't talk about work, what do you want to talk about?* Make a list of everything you can think of.

2. Then narrow it down to two or three topics.

No need to overprepare; simply use this list as a reminder of the stuff you like to talk about and use it the next time an opportunity for small talk comes up.

Now that you've got a few topics you're comfortable talking about casually, you're ready to enter into a small-talk conversation with a bit more strategy. Once you are engaged in a conversation, pay attention to how different people respond:

- When talking about news or current events, do others lean into the discussion or pivot from it?

- Do your colleagues and clients prefer to mix and mingle in a speed-networking fashion or to linger in smaller groups for longer conversations?

- Before meetings start, what are people chatting about before jumping into the formal agenda?

Here are a few topics that offer the chance to dive into details with a client, helping you build rapport and trust:

- **Vacations**. People love talking about travel: where they dream of going, where they are about to go, and especially where they've been. Sharing and asking for tips and resources is always helpful, and everyone loves a good restaurant recommendation. This also opens up the possibility of sharing pictures and anecdotes, as well as a reason to follow up after the trip to see how it went.

- **The sick kids**. When the client mentions sick family members or the flu bug hitting their house, it's OK to sign off on an email by wishing everyone a speedy recovery. You now also know more about their life and can be authentically caring about their work-life juggle.

- **College and hometown pride**. I have a client who swears that the most common conversation topic at Washington cocktail parties is college football allegiances, which quickly segues into asking where everyone is from (because in Washington, everyone comes from somewhere else). Since people love to talk about their hometown, this opens up a great follow-on game of finding out who you know in common.

Clients want to know how closely you pay attention to them, their information, and the details involved. Paying attention to small talk and using it appropriately sends the signal that you are both detail-oriented and genuinely care about others.

What's more, small talk is often the first type of interaction you'll have with a new connection. This is where the energy and excitement you bring into the conversation either opens a door or inches it shut. The one and only goal? Find a good opener that expands the conversation and then set up the next interaction.

Activity

Find your best banter by filling in the blanks that follow:

I love to talk about _____, _____, and _____ when I am in a big group and need to keep the conversation light.

I've noticed that other people around me like to talk about _____, _____, and _____, which means I need to learn more about _____.

I prefer to avoid conversations about _____ and _____. (You can't hide from all small talk, but you can gracefully pivot the conversation to a topic that is more comfortable.)

I find fun topics to discuss through these sources: _____. (Sometimes, brushing up on pop culture, current events, or television trends can help equip you with a common frame of reference before heading into a networking event.)

Knowing that I could talk about _____ all day long means I need to start a good conversation by asking _____. My second question or topic will focus on _____.

An Intentional Introduction

Small talk is great, but you can't forget to introduce yourself amidst the cocktail party banter. I'm not a fan of canned, overly rehearsed elevator pitches, as they often lack energy and cut off the conversation before it begins. However, I do believe in knowing what you want to include in a good introduction and how to easily slide it into casual conversation. Although others aren't going to pause for you to deliver your perfectly performed intro, they do at least want you to tell them your name and what you do. After all, they can't be expected to trust you in the absence of such basic details.

Activity

Let's start putting together the building blocks of your introduction:

Your name: [Remember to practice it. It gets forgotten all too often in casual, pop-up conversations]

Your work: [Firm, company, location]

What you do: [Keep it to five to ten words. Don't over-think this or try to make it sound perfect. Just find the simplest and most direct words that describe your work]

Who you help: [Describe your ideal clients]

Why you love it: [Because people like to work with people who love what they do and can share that enthusiasm]

Why you're good at it: [Remember, confidence is important]

What you do outside of work: [Offer a few activities or interests you have when you're not in the office]

You've now got the skeleton of your introduction. Try it out and see how it fits. Practice it and refine it over time; it will become more natural, and you can adapt it for particular audiences. Be sure to evolve and update it as your practice matures and your circumstances change.

Once there's some banter going between you and your clients or connections, start thinking about how you could advance the conversation to something more meaningful—something that connects your work and their business. Small talk doesn't get left behind here; rather, it becomes woven into the fabric of the relationship as you progress to business matters.

Small Talk Provides the Opportunity to Follow Up

A client of mine, Kady, reached out to me when coming home from a series of conferences with a stack of business cards (yup, those are still a thing) and a list of people to follow up with. Despite this bevy of potential opportunities, Kady felt like that stack of cards was an overwhelming burden of responsibility and had no clue where to start in following up with any amount of sincerity or in any sort of timely manner.

My advice was simple: It depends. If you had a somewhat meaningful conversation, follow up this week. If it was simply a quick *Hello* or exchange in the buffet line ("Are those scalloped potatoes?"), then a more casual connection showing appreciation for the encounter or a LinkedIn invitation request, might be more appropriate.

When you're at a conference or networking event, set a rule for yourself about who you will connect with when you get back to your desk (or on the airplane back home). Make a list of the people you met and are maybe connected to on LinkedIn, and those who don't need to be sent a perfectly crafted email the moment you get back to your normal routine.[19]

---

19 I have a specific plan for retreats and conferences that takes the guesswork out of making the most of these high-impact networking opportunities, while also allowing you to relax and enjoy the prospect of walking into the room and meeting new people. You can find it in the Toolbox.

A simple follow-up email to those you exchanged a casual conversation with is often all that's needed to move the relationship forward. Here's a simple template:[20]

> Hello [insert name],
>
> It was fantastic meeting you at [event]. I enjoyed our conversation about [reference something you talked about]. I would love the chance to continue the conversation/I look forward to connecting with you at [an event or location where you might both be next]. Please let me know what your schedule looks like for us to connect in the next couple of weeks [it is critical to put some timeframe around the next step, without seeming over-eager].
>
> I am looking forward to continuing the conversation.
>
> Thanks,
> [Your name]

Small talk is the key to so many conversations. It allows everyone to relax a bit before diving into the bigger conversations. It allows you to learn about others and lets them learn about you. It is also the gateway to getting the next conversation on the calendar.

---

20 There is no need to sit staring at your screen wondering what to say when a simple email template file can help make sure you have your emails in order, in a voice and tone that sounds like you. As you test and tweak the emails, you can make sure they are progressing the conversation the way you want them to. Said another way, make sure your emails sound like you and not me. And if you aren't getting replies, the email and approach need to change.

The lesson? The lightest of conversations often lead to the greatest of relationships. Knowing that true connections happen through shared moments of laughter. And then, you can confidently ask the next appropriate question, which is often: *Tell Me More.*

Go for It

Trust yourself to be the trusted thinking partner your clients want and need. That confidence will impress them the most.

When I graduated from the University of Michigan in 1996, my friends all grabbed big backpacks, dog-eared paperback travel guides, and Eurail passes and set out to discover the world. While they were out meeting other twentysomethings, staying in crowded hostels, and finding themselves, I left Ann Arbor and returned home to prep for law school. The story I told everyone (including myself) about why I wasn't doing the same as my friends was that my parents wouldn't let me travel without a formal program. The truth is, I never asked.[21]

To be blunt, I was too chicken to even contemplate that journey. I didn't know how to make traveling feel safe, or how to find a trusted travel partner. I was unsure of how it would work but didn't trust myself to figure it out. And so, I stayed behind, uncertain about my capacity and capability to navigate the unknown. Had I felt the support of a strong, trusted network, that would have been a game changer. This type

---

21 This was their original policy, but since my sister pulled this off effortlessly two years later, I clearly misjudged my parents.

of support is the path to not only landing that next great client, it's also an essential step on the journey to becoming a trusted thinking partner.

Before you can have the business relationships you dream about, you have to trust that you won't mess everything up as you navigate them. Trust starts with understanding and believing that you are capable of handling the opportunities that show up. It also means you can discern the best approach to advance each step and will recognize when to reach out for help. If the battered travel guide isn't enough comfort for you, grab a wing-person to travel with for this leg of the journey. Having a trusted person to bounce ideas off or walk with you into the room is often the most valuable resource you can have.

And like me with travel, you must trust yourself enough to know when you're actually nervous, and why. When the stakes are high, the nerves might just be a surge of adrenaline you feel because the good stuff is falling into place.

What to Do with the Nervous Energy

When you enter a conversation just trying to impress, you fail to connect to your own honest enthusiasm and energy. That's exactly what happened when my now husband, Andrew, met my mother, Harriet. You see, Andrew wanted to impress my mom. That made him nervous. As his nerves kicked into high gear, he tried even harder to impress her—which was having the opposite effect. In his nervousness, what Andrew forgot to do was be himself. He was desperate to impress and be likable that he created a gulf between them that shut down any possibility of getting to know one another.

My mother wasn't looking to "hire" Andrew into our family, but the challenge they had in creating a bond is the same challenge you face when setting out to build and grow great client relationships. When you enter a conversation with a prospective client, it's normal to worry about being "impressive"—coming across as put together and confident but not braggy. When you show up as guarded, everything from your first *Hello* to your pitch is charged with uncomfortable energy. Worried about a misstep, you overthink small moments. Overprepared, you don't give yourself space to take a deep breath and properly engage in the conversations that allow opportunities to unfold organically. This creates a barrier between you and your client. It's easy to spot and hard to overcome.

A better way to connect with clients starts with taking that deep breath and allowing yourself to be authentically imperfect. Setting aside the idea of perfection doesn't mean being unprepared or accepting showing up mediocre; it just means not being perfectly polished or overly rehearsed. When you're authentically imperfect, your personality, your energy, and your expertise have the space to show up and impress a client on their own, making a powerful statement to clients about how you will show up for them.

You see, nerves are a tricky business whether you are trying to find the nerve to meet a future mother-in-law, travel with friends, land the client, or be respected at the deal table. While there is much more to be said about this, taking two deep breaths and confidently engaging in the conversation helps you show up for the conversation, and eventually earn that spot as the trusted thinking partner your clients want and need. Clients aren't going to trust you to lead the team if you are standing in the back, second-guessing your own instincts, expertise, and advice, not to mention leading with awkward energy that acts as a barrier to getting to know each other.

An important decision to make at this point is to allow yourself to confidently guide your conversations and client relationships forward rather than letting your intent to impress stand in the way of action.

Activity

Let's consider how these conversations and opportunities look for you. Grab a paper and pen and set a timer for three minutes.

Think of two conversations: one that you loved and one that fell flat (or felt like a train wreck that you couldn't seem to prevent).

Compare and contrast how each conversation evolved, including the preparation and the energy behind them.

- How was the discussion set up?

- What do you notice when breaking down these discussions?

- What was the tone, tenor, and pacing of each?

- Were there awkward silences or pauses, or did the discussion flow?

Can you identify where your energy showed up well and where it didn't? Did you get worried about being impressive or getting it right? What about the other parties in the discussion?

Give Yourself Permission to Pause

Sometimes nerves and overthinking a client opportunity look like procrastination. It might take the form of not sending that next email, or not picking up the phone for fear of what might happen. Frequently, after clients describe their situation, I point out that what they're doing isn't procrastinating but stepping back. Procrastination means delaying or postponing something. Stepping back, by contrast, means taking a pause to understand the complexity of a situation and figure out the right way and moment to proceed. It is not a delay; it's taking time to figure out the next step. You move through this feeling by leaning into your trust in both you and others. Lean on all the knowledge and experience you have to lead you through tricky conversations and the weird parts of establishing a new relationship. Stepping back is looking for the strategy that works for you and will resonate with your clients.

But spending too much time staring at your screen and waiting for the perfect words to magically appear can be more wasteful than taking the next step for each conversation (and relationship). I was never going to get on that plane to Europe without some assurance that I wouldn't get lost and separated from friends; after all, this was long before cell phones could navigate every neighborhood in the world. But if someone had offered me a simple way to join in the fun while managing the risk, it would have been worth it to see the world before adult obligations stood in my way. I might have been able to relax and have a little fun.

My client, Gretchen, faced just this quandary when trying to follow up on what felt to her like the most amazing potential client she had come across in a long time. More than ideal, this client was a career-changer. As she searched for the right words to respond to the prospect's email asking about a new representation, Gretchen became overwhelmed and allowed her thoughts to take over. She started thinking things like: *What could happen?* and *What happens if I get this simple first reply wrong?* and *What were they thinking wanting to talk to* me? She felt paralyzed, and the email just wasn't getting sent. For days.

When we finally jumped on a call, and two deep breaths (seriously, just two) later, Gretchen regrouped and we quickly wrote the email together. Moments after she hit send, I received a text from Gretchen. It simply said, "They responded!" Yeah, she landed that client and more importantly, learned a great lesson when you decide that taking the next step to move the relationship forward is worth it.

This prospective client didn't need perfectly polished prose; they just wanted a follow-up and a plan for the next steps. Simple.

Allow Yourself to be Present in the Relationship

When the future of your practice depends on your book of business, the idea of relaxing in client relationships may seem quaint. The instinct may be to hold tight and micromanage, but it's far more important to simply stay calm and present. Instead of falling into reflexive responses, you need guideposts that allow you to navigate the situation more easily. This isn't about eliminating the nervous adrenaline that naturally comes when presented with what feels like a life-changing (or at least practice-altering) opportunity. It's about harnessing and channeling it to step up and meet the moment. Here are a few guideposts to consider:

1. When someone wants to learn about you, let them get to know the real you and the expertise you bring to the table. There is a way to own your awesomeness while staying humble.

2. Notice how many times you say no to a networking event, client pitch, or call. If you say no too often, you'll stop getting invited. Stepping into the room and engaging in the conversation allows you to expand your options.

3. Resist the urge to overplan. Showing up, staying open, trying new things, and simply engaging in conversation allows relationships to develop organically, aligning the energy on each side. Have some faith in the process.

4. Don't leave a networking or business development opportunity early because it's not going great at that moment. Sometimes, initiating one simple, brave conversation can turn a situation around. Save the running for when you're heading toward the next great opportunity, not when you're giving up on one.

5. When you're faced with the decision of building your own practice or continuing to work for others, bet on yourself. Figure out the next conversation that will support that bet and trust yourself to talk to those around you and move your plan forward, one step at a time.

As we discover how to build a book of business that establishes you as the trusted thinking partner for your clients, circle back to these guideposts to review them often. Make sure your everyday task list includes a reminder of these choices to help you focus on building a practice founded on incredible client relationships.

A Networking Next Step

It may feel like the strategies in this book presume you have a strong starting point, yet all it takes is one step forward from wherever your book of business and practice is right now. Leaning on the Nurture List you made in earlier chapters, now is a good time to jump back into conversations with relationships that have stalled out for one reason or another. Here are a handful of people you might consider prioritizing to rekindle a relationship:

1. **The former client**. This could be the client you used to work for whom you haven't spoken to since that deal closed years ago. You would love to reinvigorate this relationship but worry that any message you send will sound awkward at best.

2. **The client who went another direction**. This one didn't turn out the way you wanted, but you did have a great relationship with your personal client contact. Now, if only you could figure out a way to get back in the door.

3. **The client on the move**. This person seems to keep moving around the organization, and you can't pin them down to expand the work or find the right synergy to get the relationship reinvigorated.

4. **The best friend**. Your BFF from law school now works for a client who is a perfect fit for you, your expertise, and your firm's experience. You don't want to appear opportunistic and hold back from ever approaching the subject of what they could be looking for.

5. **The one-time email**. These are the outreaches you have already made in response to an introduction or a meeting at an event, but after that one email, you have no idea what to do next. The longer you wait, the more stale things feel, the harder it gets to re-engage, and the more you need some way to move the conversation along.

You get the picture. These aren't necessarily high-stakes conversations, but connections that also happen to align with your practice and goals. They are high-impact conversations that don't require much strategy, just a simple reach out to say *Hello*.

Trusting Yourself Doesn't Require a Trust Fall

Deciding you're ready to take a leap of faith and turn your conversations and connections into real opportunities requires that you trust yourself, and allow clients to get to know and trust you. It may feel like a tactical blend of expertise, experience, mindset, and the maturity of your practice, yet it's ultimately about how you share your expertise and show up for clients when they need you the most. We've covered how to trust yourself, some rules about choosing your words, and how to get organized enough to get you moving. Now there's one more thing that must happen before you can truly get started.

You need to have faith in everyone else because building a practice isn't done on your own. It requires interaction with and the commitment of others. There might be a long list of past experiences, both real and perceived, that have led you to conclude that nobody else is to be trusted. When it comes to colleagues, for instance, you might be challenged with:

- Others who routinely do not share origination,

- Colleagues who cling to the client relationship and restrict how you interact with and nurture the client, failing to share in the growth of new projects or opportunities, and

- The worry that others don't think you're ready, savvy enough, or the right person for the job. This is typically a byproduct of you choosing to stand on the sidelines and let others dismiss your presence or forget about your contributions to the client and the conversations.

While I could go down a rabbit hole exploring the mindset needed to overcome all of this, for now, it is important just to get centered on what is real and what is simply your reaction to the unknown. After taking a couple of deep breaths, focus on what you know to be facts. Then, decide today that you will focus on building relationships that you can have faith in. Set aside all the worries of getting left behind or cut out of the deal. Today, we move forward from a place of grounded trust.

Just as you must have faith in your colleagues, you also must have faith in your clients. Again, there could be a host of reasons, real or perceived, why you may be skeptical of them.

For example:

- The client is often slow in getting back to you, and you assume they are ghosting you, moving the work in-house, or have found an expert they like more than you.

- You didn't get a great vibe from them the last two times you saw them.

- You assume that because they have counsel they have relied on for years, nothing is going to change that relationship until there is a shift in management or a retirement.

- The rumor is that they are contemplating bringing everyone in-house, which makes it seem like a useless exercise to go after work that will never materialize.

Take two deep breaths. Then, two more. Learning to trust your clients is going to take a bit more faith, both in yourself and the others involved. Taking a more rational view of these situations:

- If they didn't want to speak to you, they wouldn't be at the lunch or event, or taking your call.

- Clients are humans like you and have stuff going on, so when they get busy, it's as forgivable as when you are busy and stuff slips.

- Clients believe in putting together the best advisors for themselves, their teams, and their company priorities. By engaging with you, they think you might be one of those team members.

- You are standing on even ground with everyone else at the table.

Authentic trust requires a mutual commitment to the relationship. Both parties need to know how to help each other succeed and how to ask for what they want and need. Being reasonable and honest with your clients is critical. Realize that being open to ideas and comfortable with someone else's solutions is often more complicated than we'd like to admit.

The reality is, decisions are often more complicated by the time they reach the decision-makers and leaders who seek legal advice. And those decision-makers are often aided by having other advisors lend an ear and help them work through the options. Clients look for a team with a deep bench in the areas they need support in, and an approach that aligns with the pace and decisions on their desk. Being available, responsive, and approachable for small, silly questions, complicated messes, and everything in between allows you to be the trusted thinking partner who gets brought in over and over again. They also want to know you are interested in being a part of their team.

Choose to Stay on the Journey

I wasn't ready for that European vacation some 20 years ago. But I began writing this book at 30,000 feet on my way to Madrid, traveling alone, and ready to discover what was out there. I didn't stay in hostels, but neither did I have a perfectly planned itinerary before landing. I wandered. I met new people. And now, believing that there is more out there when you put yourself out into the world, I engaged in incredible conversations, practicing the strategies in this book. A key note to take with you as we move from landing the client to deepening the relationship with them is to shift your focus from how you show up to how you can better understand everyone else. This is where you can rise to the challenge of being that trusted resource, the problem-solver, the one who really gets it, by paying attention and reading the room.

What's the adult version of "not getting on the plane to Europe"? It's waiting for clients to call you while telling yourself that you're doing everything you can to get your name out there; it's telling yourself they'll call when they need you, that it's a long game that requires you to keep planting seeds, hoping that one day it will all work out. With respect, that is no different than me telling everyone that my parents wouldn't let me go to Europe, without ever asking if I could.

Part Two

Trusted Thinking Partner Conversations

Building Conversations that Make Sense for Your Clients

Becoming your client's trusted partner is a series of expanding conversations that unfold one at a time.

There are few things I love more than throwing on some music, lining my kitchen counter with ingredients, and putting together an incredible pot of soup. While each pot is a bit different, the base of ingredients is always the same: an onion, celery, carrots, and stock. Depending on the consistency I am looking for, I might add cream or flour to the mix, and building a flavor profile influences which spices I reach for. Who I've got coming for dinner that night might dictate whether it goes vegetarian, or if chicken, turkey, or stew meat makes the cut. Finally, it's time to decide what will best round out the flavor and texture: vegetables, pasta, rice, or maybe matzo balls?

While every pot of soup is unique, each is created through a series of core decisions I make each time I go into soup-making mode. The same is true for how you become a trusted thinking partner. By bringing the same principles to a relationship, you will be better able to understand the other party's particularities and unique needs and bring out the full "flavor" of the relationship.

What are these principles? They include:

- Showing up for the conversation and being present

- Allowing your business knowledge to shine through while being curious about your client's position, perspective, and expertise

- Meeting your clients where they are (both physically and in the virtual world)

- Consistently following through and following up on next steps

- Offering support when it's asked for, and when you spot the need

- Devoting the same energy to nurturing the relationship with the client as you do to the tasks and projects you complete for them

These principles allow you to show up and consider the client's personality, their particular goals, and where you're speaking with them as you choose the tone and tenor of the conversation (for example, the topics you discuss at a formal dinner will be different from those in a video meeting). If you consistently bring them to bear in every conversation, you will be building the foundation for a thinking partnership, not just selling your services. A business development strategy that has conversations at its core, paired with a strategic understanding of how to advance them one step at a time, allows you to grow your client relationships by leaps and bounds.

The Relationship Foundation

The following steps and stages build the solid foundation of the conversations needed to get yourself into the role of trusted thinking partner with a current (or prospective) client.

Once you move past small talk, it's time to start really learning about the client. This stage demands that you focus more on others than yourself. Don't be in a rush to prove your expertise to the client or worry too much about impressing them. If you're attentive to the bigger picture and stay focused on the client and their priorities, you'll build trust and signal that this is a relationship you are invested in. In a sense, you are becoming less worried about proving your worth and becoming more relationship-centric.

As you learn about the client, you'll be able to clearly articulate their worries, concerns, and priorities, and this is how you move to a deeper advisory level with the relationship. To get to this place, ask good questions and pay attention to the answers and to the client's broader thoughts and perspectives. By collecting this knowledge, you become ready to share your experience and expertise in conversations with clients, as well as use this expanded understanding to amplify your expertise with a wider audience. (We'll talk more about pairing our conversation strategy and thought leadership later on in the book.) While it's a useful phrase at all stages, at this point in the relationship, it is particularly useful to ask the client: *Tell Me More*.

Each conversation you have leads to a better understanding of your clients and colleagues and a deeper understanding of your niche, all of which build additional layers of trust.

To facilitate the kind of conversations that will expand your knowledge of your client, it helps to understand which conversations energize you and allow you to best connect with clients.

Activity

Think about the types of conversations you have with your clients. Consider each scenario listed below and rank them from 1 to 10 (1 being the highest confidence, 10 being the lowest confidence) based on how you feel about entering a conversation with a client that is focused on:

- Small talk and casual banter at a networking event

- Sharing your background and expertise

- Introducing yourself

- Introducing other members of the firm

- Actively learning about clients and their priorities

- Pivoting a conversation from casual to business

- Talking about substantive issues

- Sharing your expertise (for example, giving a talk or webinar about a niche topic of interest to your clients)

- Following up and following through with clients regarding a prospective new matter

- Closing the deal

After you've ranked each scenario, note those you feel most confident with. Do you notice any patterns? What about those scenarios you aren't as confident about? Do you tend to avoid the low-confidence scenarios? Take notes on each, as we refer to these conversations throughout the book.

There is no "right" or "wrong" on the scale you've completed above—rather, this exercise is meant to give you some perspective on where your energy and confidence intertwine at the different stages of business development conversations. This exercise is also *not* giving you permission to skip out on the stages of the conversation you don't love. Instead, it's showing you how to recognize your own personal "sticking points" in the conversation and find better ways to engage with them in a way that works for you.

The Thinking Partner Conversation Strategy

Now that you and your client know each other, your conversation strategy moves toward providing expertise, experience, and wisdom that positions you as the thinking partner. These stages are often more about small, everyday moments than big, sweeping gestures.[22] This comes in the form of

---

22 There is, however, one important situation where it pays to deliver a big, sweeping gesture. Giving a pitch for business, when you're invited to do so, requires a different level of preparation and practice. While much of the preparation for pitches involves putting together a packet of materials (possibly a PowerPoint summary of your expertise) and framing a competitive pricing model, there is far more work to be done that acknowledges the important issues facing the potential client and how your approach aligns with their priorities.

sending helpful alerts and information to your clients or noticing and forwarding a news story that might impact their priorities. It comes as an invitation to an event or to a roundtable discussion with other industry players. It's simple and best with no strings attached.

From here, the path forward is simply to share knowledge and ideas that resonate with clients. You know they will resonate because it's based on information you've gathered from being present and engaged. Then, you follow up and follow through on your commitments from those conversations.

What does "following through" mean in this context? To put it bluntly, if you say you're going to send something over, send it; if you offer to make an introduction, make that introduction; if the client wants you to bring your team over to brainstorm, show up with your team and brainstorm. This is where keeping your word determines whether you're the client's thinking partner or simply a resource for a particular project.

Once you've laid the foundation of trust, the next step to becoming a trusted thinking partner is spotting areas where the client has *not* asked you for help but where you could help them and offering to contribute there too. This should not be over-eagerness or a slimy pitch for more work. Rather, it's you making sure that the client knows you're invested in their success. This next step in the conversation could be as simple as sharing an article that speaks to an issue they're facing, collaborating with the client to develop a training session, or making plans to have the next conversation about the issue.

Once You Get the Meeting, Prepare

Getting ready for a conversation involves asking yourself, your colleagues, and your clients a series of questions. These include:

- Is there anything in particular that you need to know before the meeting?

- Does the client want to focus the conversation on anything specific?

- Who else are they working with?

- Does anyone in your network have experience in this particular subject matter or industry?

- What are the latest trends in the subject matter or industry and/or has the client organization been hit with any press recently, either positive or negative?

- Does the client want to meet the whole team, or are there specific people from the firm that you should bring to the meeting?

Ask, Don't Assume

One of the main reasons why pitches and relationships fall apart at this initial phase is because you let your assumptions about what the client is looking for obscure their actual wants and needs. A much better approach, with a higher likelihood of success, is to ask the client, directly and upfront, what they're looking for. But before you pick up the phone, list out the questions you have, what you think they might want to learn (or what you know and wish to confirm from a more formal request), and who you need to bring to the conversation.[23] A pre-planning meeting or two can go a long way toward calming your nerves and recognizing a great, trusted partnership in the making.[24]

A reminder here that client development strategies (including your conversation approach) work best when your whole team is on the same page. Knowing that everyone understands the building blocks of the conversations and what you are learning about the client as a whole allows you to deepen your collective understanding of the dynamics, priorities, and relationships throughout the client team. This allows your firm to truly be the trusted partner.

Guide the Conversation

Years ago, through a coaching assignment in which I had to learn to knit, I was given the challenge of learning to slow down. After hours of effort that produced a seemingly endless tangle of knots and ugly, frayed edges, I sought help at the neighborhood knitting store. The woman at the shop asked me to show her what I had done to create such a mess. After I'd attempted a few more clumsy knots, she asked me to stop. Apparently, my grip on the yarn was so tight that it was breaking. Her advice has stuck with me ever since:

> If you want to create something, guide it in your hand and allow it to develop. If you clench too tightly to the result, it will have no choice but to break.

---

23 One important note: If you can find the information you need from a quick Google search, then it's not a question you should be bringing to the client team. Doing your homework shines through right here.

24 The Toolbox has a conversation planning sheet to help you get in the habit of mapping out such conversations up front.

That same precept is essential in building authentically strong client relationships. If you try to leap directly from *Hello* to a signed engagement letter, forcing the matter and clinging on desperately, you will break the relationship before it begins. To create a relationship that lasts, guide it by following through on the conversation progression...over and over again.

Build a System of Outstanding Client Relationships

The nature of private practice is that you are constantly cultivating client relationships. You do not want to build only one client relationship; you want to build a portfolio of client relationships. That is what your practice growth depends on. To build that kind of book, you need a system.

With a plethora of relationships to consider (colleagues, community, clients), establishing a system for nurturing all of them, especially clients, is key. You don't know which of your connections is going to turn into that Ideal further down the road. The key to a strong practice is to have several layers of clients. Some will be cornerstone clients that you have a deep relationship with, while others will be starting to trust you and your team as advisors. Your goal is to have a balance of clients across these layers of depth and in terms of size.

Activity

Take a piece of paper and split it into three sections:

1. In one section, make a list of the clients you have worked with the longest (regardless of size). These are the clients who continuously call you or request that you join the team for a project or case.

2. Next, list your biggest clients in the second section. These are the clients you have done the most work for over the past year.

3. In the third section, list those clients that have sent you a project or two, but keep talking about finding ways to bring you more.

When you look at the results of the exercise above, you will realize that your practice already has layers of clients in place. The strategies in this book are intended to nurture that network as a whole, as well as the clients within each of those levels. And each strategy begins with the simple yet profound act of showing up for the conversation in an open, genuine way.

As we've discussed in this chapter, over-planning and focusing too intently on the outcome you're hoping for often leads to awkward exchanges, or even a total failure to engage with a client. Once you recognize how many of the building blocks of a relationship derive from random, unplanned, everyday moments, you can allow yourself the space to be spontaneous, attentive, and responsive. By doing this, you'll start to truly know the client, how they work, what they care about, and how you can support them as they pursue their goals. This is the next step on the road to becoming a trusted thinking partner.

Be Relationship-Centric

*Trusted thinking partners
have a growth mindset about
the possibilities waiting within
good client relationships.*

Whether she was entertaining family, friends, or clients, my mother had a knack for making everything look a bit fancier than it was, even if the setting was casual and comfortable. She could tuck a piece of fine silverware into a paper picnic napkin in a way that just seemed natural.

I recall the time she brought an annual client appreciation event into our home. Mom planned an evening that was fancy from the start: a private chef, a pianist accompanying dinner, and beautiful wines. But what made the evening truly memorable was what happened at the end of the night. Before the event finished, guests were invited into the kitchen. Piled in every corner of the room were cookies of all kinds, which she had baked herself from recipes handed down over the years. Each guest received a bag in which they were encouraged to stash as many cookies as they wished. The camaraderie and conversation that ensued as everyone eagerly sampled the cookies, filled their bags, and marveled at the transformed space was priceless.

By arranging this twist on the traditional holiday cookie exchange, my mother wasn't only thinking of how to end the night on a perfect note but also of how the clients would carry that feeling with them after they walked out the door. Even as she was planning the event, she'd been thinking about the conversations that would come after it and grow out of it. This is the difference between traditional networking and creating a chain of conversations that expands a relationship. The latter will have a beginning, but when thoughtful in its approach and informed by a genuine interest in others, it will often have no absolute end.

This chapter is focused on what happens after clients walk in the door and teaches you to draw on more than your expertise alone to attract clients. At this point, you need to consider how you can attract clients by reading the room and how to make a client not only feel comfortable working with you but also trust that you get them and the project.

Set the Stage for Success

A client of mine—let's call her Brooke—told me about an opportunity she had to pitch to someone she considered an incredible Ideal. She knew she had an easier time conversing with clients over a meal, so she decided to recreate a dining experience for the pitch meeting right there in her office. This wasn't just bagels in boxes. On the morning of the meeting, the conference room was completely transformed with fine linens, silverware, and a piping hot breakfast.

The care that Brooke put into this setting said more about her to the client than a pitch booklet ever could. Before she even began the conversation, Brooke had signaled what the client could expect from her as counsel and as a thinking partner. She literally set the (breakfast) table, which set the stage for success.

You don't need to recreate a formal dining setting every time you meet a client for an initial conversation. Some clients will want to be taken to that new restaurant everyone is talking about, others are just looking for a great cup of coffee and a comfortable chair, while others will want to skip the dishes altogether in favor of a meticulous, formal presentation. In every case, the key is to read the room. In other words, drop any assumptions about what you *think* will make your practice shine for the client and pay attention to how the client *wants* to be treated.

Activity

Identify an opportunity to network with someone from your Nurture List in the coming weeks. Ask yourself:

1. Are they more formal or relaxed?

2. Do they appreciate a conversation that is all business from the start? Or one that gets there eventually after lengthy small talk?

3. Where do you shine in connecting with others? At a large networking event? Meeting in a conference room? In a coffee shop?

4. Where do the client's or colleague's energy and approach align with yours?

Use this as a starting point to pick an approach that feels comfortable for you and aligned with your client. The next step is to reach out to get the meeting on the calendar.

Focusing Farther Down the Path

While I am adamant about not focusing too intently on the outcome of the relationship before you even get it off the ground, it's still useful to consider how you want the client relationship to progress in the long term. A brief pause at the beginning to envision what might come next is a valuable use of your time.

Walking into that initial conversation with the end in mind is part preparation (you've researched the client), part organization (you've created an agenda or checklist of points to discuss), and part mindset (you've grounded your energy to focus on—and be attentive to—the people you are meeting). It's this last one that is most often overlooked, and when neglected, it can put the end in jeopardy right from the outset.

Consider this example: you have a pitch conversation at 3 p.m. You see from your calendar that you have back-to-back meetings until 2:30, and you also know you need to find time to get back to some clients on pressing matters. You scramble to join the video call at 2:59. (Deep breath? No time. Glass of water? You'll grab one later.) You're frantic, and hope the rest of the team joins soon and is more organized than you are.

The alternative: you have a pitch conversation at 3 p.m. You check in with the team first thing in the morning to compare notes after yesterday's run-through. You've blocked your calendar from 2:30 to 3 p.m., but double-check to make sure nothing has popped up unexpectedly—all clear. At 2:30, you shut your email and take a short walk, hitting the restroom and grabbing some water (possibly even some fresh air). Before you log into the video meeting, you pause for a few deep breaths. You're calm, centered, and entirely focused on how you want to feel at the end of the call. Confident, you sign in.

How would you expect these two pitches to go? Flying in at the last minute and squeezing it into your day? Or calmly, confidently bringing together the all-star team, focused and ready to engage with new clients? I can tell you who I would want to work with. How about you?

Practice Polite Persistence

Once you've initiated the client relationship and have a view in your mind about where you want it to lead, the next step is to strategize about how to properly pace that relationship and build consistent trust along the way. On the one hand, you don't want the client to feel like you're constantly badgering them for more business by sending them an avalanche of emails and voicemails. On the other hand, you don't want to come across as nonchalant and uninterested in the client and their problems. An obligatory holiday card once a year and a handshake at an annual industry conference are all good, but they're not sufficient for building a true thinking partnership.

One of the most common questions I'm asked is how to communicate with clients and keep the conversation going. Once again, reading the room (that is, understanding the preferences of each and every unique and particular client) is crucial to setting the right pace for both you and the client.

That said, there are a few guidelines that you can apply to nearly every situation:

1. **Initial contact**. When you meet someone, send a simple *Hello* with your contact information within the first couple of days. Waiting any longer might make it seem like you forgot.

2. **Request for information**. When a client or prospect asks for materials from you, send them over promptly.

3. **Follow up**. If you haven't heard back from the client or prospect after a week, send a simple follow-up email to make sure they received it. If you don't hear back right after this, just relax; the emails may yet work their magic without you having to push too hard.

4. **Touch base**. If you still haven't heard from the client or prospect after six to 12 weeks, send over an article or item of interest along with a cheerful note about connecting soon. This can bump you back to the top of their mind without it seeming like you're nagging.

There is one very simple way to know when you should reach out to a client: ask them. Don't be shy about talking timing with clients and colleagues, especially in the early conversations. Clarity comes from a clear, agreed-upon timeline and clear expectations around follow-up and is usually appreciated by clients. In fact, it can even build greater trust. Pacing a relationship (and each individual conversation) is more about keeping in line with client expectations than trying to hurry everyone along. While some suggest that patience is a virtue, in a business development strategy, it's about matching the pace (fast or slow) so that you're ready when the client says, "Go!"

Activity

Pick one colleague or client you keep in touch with regularly, and answer the following questions:

1. How do you typically communicate with them? Email, text, in-person, phone, or video conference?

2. How often do you connect with them besides giving project updates?

3. Are you hearing back from this person promptly, or are there gaps in the conversation? (This is often a clue to whether you're aligned in your pacing.)

4. How do they reply? By the same method you used to reach out, or are they picking up a phone to reply to emails (for example)? It is useful to align with their approach.

Now, pick someone you want to develop a relationship with or deepen the work you do for or with them, and ask the same four questions. There might be some details here that you need to learn more about. Consider this information to get more curious about as you look to expand the work from that one project to many.

Building on Everyday Moments to Deepen the Client Relationships You Already Have

I often think of my mother and her penchant for creating memorable experiences. By orchestrating that lovely cookie party in her kitchen to top off a wonderful evening with clients, she was also creating a way for clients to reach out the next day to share which were their favorite cookies and continue the conversation through the weeks and months ahead. She was strategic and intentional with this plan. Trust-building doesn't only happen in one-on-one conversations. The journey continues as you explore where and how else you send signals and messages to your clients. These communicate that you are not only present for their conversations, but also that your approach and presence are consistent, predictable, and reliable.

Ask a Good Question

*Thinking partners know
how to ask a question and
hold space for the answer.*

When I was choosing a pediatrician for my children, all the lawyers in my office pointed me to the same doctor they all saw for their kids. When asked what made this one doctor incredible, their answers were consistent and clear:

> "He is even-keeled and calm."

> "He knows when to raise the worry flag and when to help you take a deep breath."

> "He asks good questions, and his expertise results in really good care for your kids."

What they were saying was: You can trust this doctor to be your pediatric thinking partner. I called the office right away and was added to his patient roster. He remained our trusted partner for years until, unfortunately (for us), he retired.

This is the same approach lawyers need to take to become a trusted thinking partner for their clients:

- Stay calm when the client is frantic.

- Raise the worry flag when necessary.

- Help clients take a deep breath and sit with them until they can find calm.

- Ask better questions to guide your advice to clients or to navigate the strategic choices they're considering.

- Use your expertise to advance your clients' goals and solve their problems (not just show them off for everyone to see).

Simply being curious about your clients is arguably the most effective strategy for building strong client relationships, but it's also often the most misunderstood. The reason for this is that it is often over-simplified as merely "getting to know" clients. But "getting to know" feels amorphous because it ignores the little problem of knowing what to ask them about.

If you're worried you'll need to spend hours creating a long list of questions to memorize, don't fret; we're going to start with just a few good ones.

Building a Better Question

When I said you need to get curious about your clients and what's going on with them, your mind may have jumped to simple questions like:

- "What are you working on?"
- "What are you worried about?"
- "What keeps you up at night?"
- "How do you anticipate growing next year?"

While well-intentioned, these questions often beget unhelpful responses:

Question: "What are you working on?"
Answer: "Cleaning out my emails."

Question: "What are you worried about?"
Answer: "Getting treats to my kid's classroom."

Question: "What keeps you up at night?"
Answer: "My husband's snoring."

Question: "How do you anticipate growing next year?"
Answer: "I'm just trying to stay afloat."

However, these dead ends can be avoided with some strategic stage-setting. A smidge of context can elicit greater direction and focus on clients' responses. For example:

> *I'm working on a client alert intended to help people understand [insert update, tricky concept, common question about your practice], and I'm wondering: which part of it often causes the most problems for you and your team?*

When you ask which part of the topic clients are concerned about, you give them an opening to engage with you and help them understand the point of your question. It lets you communicate your knowledge and expertise without making a big show of it. This is a trust-builder for clients wanting to be sure that the important issues will rise to the top with you.

Next, you might continue with another question, such as: "How are you and your team talking about [update/concept/common question]?"

Now you have asked the first strategic question that will progress the conversation. You've also left the door open to learn more about the client's priorities (rather than assuming that you know what they are or should be). This is one more step toward infusing trust into the relationship.

Good Questions are More Efficient

Years ago, I was asked to lead a book club for a women's group at a law firm. A committee had met and decided that a quarterly book club was an excellent way to bring the firm's women together, and they wanted me to head it up.

I had two questions: "Have you asked anyone whether they want a book club?" and "Will anyone actually attend?" The silence was deafening. I was then told that the committee had decided it was a great idea. It quickly became clear that the committee had made this decision in a vacuum and that we had to actually talk to the women they wanted to show up and engage them in designing the program.[25]

Pivoting the conversation, I told them that to frame the program appropriately, they would need to ask the members of the larger group some simple questions about the group's goals, the book club concept, and what they wanted to get out of it. Within a few days, it became clear that while the committee itself might show up to the book club, that was

---

25 A super-important note here about book clubs. What tends to work well for law firms, affinity groups, and other book-centric gatherings is a book *talk*. Unlike traditional book *clubs*, these don't require anyone to read a book in advance, study a text, or feel ill-prepared when they join their colleagues for a conversation. Speaking of book talks, I love to lead and participate in them, both with my own books and other books that I love sharing with others.

about it. Among the wider group, the attitude was that the pressures of their everyday responsibilities meant they were unlikely to be able to sneak away for a book club meeting, let alone read the book.

With this understanding of what the group actually wanted, we recast the book club as a pop-up workshop: no reading or prep required. This low-pressure variant proved successful and resulted in a great conversation for everyone who attended. By listening carefully to the group, we were able to create a sense of community and gained the respect and participation of the members.

To take a wider view of this principle: when you build out a program, work product, or business model without validating that it will be valuable for your Ideals, you deploy a "fingers-crossed" strategy. This is not the way to build the thriving book of business you desire.

You Just Need One Question

Much of the focus of business development is on getting in front of clients at networking events or angling to get the "right" people at the table for a business dinner. Yet while getting the work is the ultimate goal, often little time is spent on the simple but crucial everyday connection points. You could keep rambling on about your work and your firm's capabilities (making sure to cite that latest appeals-court case, of course) as a way to connect with your client, but there is another strategy that yields a much better conversation: ask one good question.

Crafting a great question requires as much time and consideration as deciding which restaurant to meet at for lunch.

But giving yourself a plan and direction for the conversation at that lunch allows you to actively navigate it with your clients, rather than simply throwing expertise at them and hoping it's impressive enough to get you hired.

Some questions that deepen the conversation and are grounded in everyday moments are:

- "What are your near-term priorities to navigate the current economy?"

- "Can you explain to me how you've seen business and legal teams most effectively negotiate together?"

- "Now that you are in-house, what do you wish you knew when you were outside counsel?"

These questions are simple conversation expanders and signal that you are interested and care about the client. When you ask one good question, you extend the conversation and expand what you know about the client and their priorities. This knowledge will positively impact how you work with them and the nature of the work you do together.

A strategic question also allows you to take on the role of the researcher through your conversations by asking a handful of clients, colleagues, or referral partners the same question and comparing answers to pick up on common themes.

There's incredible value to be gained from this: the client's word choices and the energy they bring to the topic signal their perspective and approach; these are cues you need to pay attention to. If you miss this opportunity, the client will assume (correctly, in this instance) that you weren't paying attention or don't care. If they keep talking about the practical application of a regulation, and you focus on the legal intricacies because that's where your expertise lies, then you're missing the mark. This runs the risk of breaking your trusted relationship with the client and forcing you to move into repair mode (a space that isn't impossible to escape but is often not fun to be in).

A client of mine, Michelle, needed to find a strategy to highlight her expertise in a way that would advance conversations with potential clients. She planned to continue to use client alerts as a business development tool, but she first wanted to understand how they were used both internally (by her colleagues) and externally (by the clients and prospects). The old approach was to send alerts and hope they were viewed as valuable. They were always appreciated, but not the business generator Michelle was hoping for.

To improve on this, we repositioned client alerts to become conversation starters, which offered a helpful tool to prompt the next client conversation. The key to this was asking clients the question: "How do you use alerts, and what's the most helpful information (and format) for you to receive in this environment of constant change?" Using client alerts to touch base with potential clients allowed Michelle to put herself in the position of building trust and respect for her expertise. It also allowed her to be the leader in a bigger conversation.

The way that Michelle's one good question could be framed in a client conversation might be:

> *I'm working on a project to simplify client alerts and put them together to be efficient and effective for you and your team. Can you tell me where you spend most of your time looking for industry updates and what you like most about the updates you receive?*

By contrast, framing the same question for an internal audience might be more along the lines of:

- "How much information belongs in the client alerts, and what should be part of a bigger conversation with the clients individually?"

- "How are we sending these out to make sure the decision-makers see the updates?"

- "Also, where is the line drawn between billable hours and the non-billable updates that shine a light on the practice group's expertise?"

The cool thing about this strategy is that there are endless possibilities and opportunities to forge connections and conversations with clients and potential clients. Each attorney has their own question that is appropriate and supportive for their practice and business development goals. In addition, if a question isn't working, change it. If you aren't getting the answers you were expecting, consider the clients and your approach to the topic to see which needs to change first.

Activity

How do you find that first question?

Imagine you're at the top industry conference. Instead of heading into the current session (which you heard was boring), you're sitting in the hall at a table full of Ideals. The conversation is invigorating, with clients and colleagues all brainstorming and bantering about the latest hot topics in the field.

1. Make a list of all the topics that might come up in this energetic conversation.

2. Now, think of a question you could ask three to five people from that table that would elicit a different perspective or conversation from each one. (Reminder: The more general the question, the less valuable the information you gather might be.)

Test your question out with someone and see how it goes.

Listen More, Talk Less

Now that you see how a strategic question opens the door, you must listen carefully to the answers. When you ask an interesting question, you give the other person the chance to share their perspective, expertise, and experience; you give them the spotlight and give yourself the opportunity to learn. Now is not the time to tell a client they're wrong or that they don't get it. It's also not the time to jump in with your expertise to prove your worth. Rather, it's a time to talk less and listen more by asking them to *Tell Me More*.

Tell Me More is a transition point in a conversation. It gives the client permission to "keep going" to expand on the ideas and perspectives they're sharing with you. More details and background often come to the surface at this stage and through this prompt. You're holding space in the conversation by listening and waiting your turn to ask further, clarifying questions. This engenders a deeper layer of trust that the best relationships have at their foundation.

Expanding the conversation, and by extension the client relationship, with a good question or two signals that you're interested in the other party, willing to support them at a much deeper level, and not just grasping for that next billable hour. You're willing to set your ego aside and learn about their perspectives and plans. This is the secret sauce to how you create the value they want and need.

Let's pause to reflect on where you are so far in moving a relationship from advisor to thinking partner. You progressed from small talk and moved the conversation one step forward by asking a good question and learning more about the client. You paid close attention in the conversation and gave yourself an excuse to follow up (and, of course, follow through, for example, by creating the client alert you brainstormed together), and came away with a better understanding of how others see an issue that is important to you.

When you ask a good question, the insights you glean allow you to deepen the relationship as you provide valuable advice and work products that better resonate with clients. Furthermore, it signals to them that you understand what they want and are invested in their success.

Merge into the Conversation

Joining the conversation is half the battle. The rest is staying interested and engaged.

My daughter danced in *The Nutcracker* with the Kansas City Ballet Company for nine seasons. That meant nine years of driving a carpool filled with student performers. To make all this time behind the wheel worthwhile, I would take the opportunity to teach a new life lesson to the young girls piled into the car. The most popular lesson, still discussed by many of those girls, is how to pull out of the parking garage. When trying to exit the garage after a performance, many drivers would struggle to work up the gumption to stick their noses out and claim their rightful place on the road. The lesson? Take your turn when it is offered, and "own your merge."

This is a balance of safety and courage. Hesitating means losing your chance and having to wait for another opening. Barging out too fast can lead to a collision. But, by paying attention and reading the non-verbal cues from other drivers, when it's your turn, you can safely and confidently go.

This lesson has many applications, not least when it comes to client relationships and your conversations, which require a similar balance of safety and courage. While you shouldn't burst into a client conversation with a barrage of questions, it can also be tempting to play it too safe, give the client space, and hope they'll call when they're ready. However, if you're ready to be the trusted thinking partner, when you spot that opening, don't just poke your front bumper in and hope space will open up—pay attention, read the cues, and go. This puts you in the driver's seat and allows you to learn more about the client, their focus, their needs, and ways you can expand your opportunities together. The key is to find that opening.

Openings can arise at any stage of a conversation. The following are a few examples of how this plays out in different parts of a client relationship:

1. **Joining small talk**. You find the courage to show up and join the discussion where your client or prospect hangs out. You walk up to the group and join the discussion. In dating terms, you made the first move.

2. **Converting small talk into something more**. Now you turn your small talk into a business conversation in a way that feels natural but still moves the conversation forward. This progression requires a bit more practice and intention, which is why it is often the one most avoided.

3. **Deepening an existing relationship**. At this point, both sides of a client relationship are waiting for the other side to make a move that expands the conversation into something deeper. The issue is that this is

rarely communicated explicitly but instead shows up as a work question, a brainstorm, or a side conversation ready for your engagement.

Consider the case of Beatrice, one of my clients. Beatrice is an excellent attorney, known throughout the community for her work and for supporting other lawyers. She is constantly networking. At lunch one day, she was talking to a fellow lawyer who had gone in-house. This lawyer was known as an advocate for women in law. She shared her disappointment that her strong network of women lawyers had not reached out to find out how they might support her in the new role. In fact, she wondered why they hadn't pitched her for work in her new role. Beatrice recognized an opening when she heard it and started asking the other lawyer about what she was looking for in outside counsel. She also talked about the resources she could provide. What Beatrice learned was that she had to make it known that she wanted to be considered for the work. She decided to "own the merge" and make herself part of the bigger client conversation.

The question that inevitably comes up next is: *How do you make the request to be included?* Asking flat out feels as awkward as asking someone out on a date when you're not sure how they feel about you. You want that next move to be smooth, not sales-y. You want to frame it so you won't cut yourself off from future opportunities if you've read the room wrong.

Here are a few ways to approach such a conversation:

- "I would love the opportunity to get involved the next time you have a project like this on your desk."

- "We would love to be considered for the next project/ case/deal."

- *"Tell Me More* about how we might work together."

- *"Tell Me More* about what might be most useful for you and your team."

Powerful Tools to Guide the Conversation

To invoke the greatest conversation strategy out there once again, *Tell Me More* works wonderfully at this crucial stage in the conversation. It invites the client to share more about their priorities and position without overstepping. At this point in the conversation, you need to learn more, and the best way to do this is to give the client the floor. *Tell Me More* lets you guide the conversation while it naturally expands at the pace and in the direction that suits the client. What they choose to expand on are breadcrumbs that lead to the priorities they care about.

For example, if the conversation expands from "Managing legal contracts is such a headache" to "All these agreements are creating a tracking nightmare," then you understand this is a volume issue. Then, the help they need may be in discerning how to organize the agreements. By contrast, if the conversation morphs into "The time and attention needed to get the contracts right is slowing us down," then you understand that timing is the issue. And if the conversation expands to "The people negotiating the agreements don't have the judgment needed to make a decision," the opening is yours to help them fill this judgment gap. Just opening the door to learning and seeing the ways you can help all starts with *Tell Me More*.

This example demonstrates how the clues in a conversation help you guide the discussion until you're able to identify how you can provide value to the client. It naturally creates opportunity for you in a sophisticated, not sales-y way.

There are three big clues hiding in this type of conversation:

1. **Understanding the client**. What they care about matters. How they choose to expand the conversation tells you much about their understanding of the topic, the headaches it's giving them, and how deep they want to go with the conversation.

2. **Opportunity to follow up**. When a client or colleague tells you more about a subject, it often opens the door for you to offer to help.

3. **Social clues**. You read that right—not cues, but clues. Think of networking like a great game, and it becomes a whole lot more fun. The clues the client drops in the conversation allow you to learn about what's working with their current team, what's stressing them out, what they want someone else to handle, and what they could geek out on all day long. That last one is key: if they're interested in a subject, it's easy to engage with them and find the energy to expand the conversation.

Make sure to take notes on the clues you find when you pause and consider the conversations.

Activity

Brainstorm all the topics that are of interest to a client or colleague with whom you'd like to move further into a business conversation. Questions that can help with this brainstorm include:

- What are the topics they're required to focus on as part of their job?

- What conversations always seem to be coming up when you're with them?

- What topics do you think they need to focus on that are rarely brought up?

Out of these lists, pick two to three to start with and use them as guideposts to anchor the conversation and move it forward.

Tell Me More naturally transitions to the next great door opener: *Can I Suggest?*

Can I Suggest? asks the client's permission for you to offer them ideas and advice. It allows you to understand when they are venting and when they are open to support and gives you an idea of how wide the opening is for you to step in as the trusted advisor.

Merging the Casual Conversation into Business

Now that you have decided to head into a business conversation, you need a few ways to continue guiding the conversation toward that. Often, this type of transition can happen easily in the small, everyday moments.

Here are some examples:

- "OK, since we're talking about [current small-talk topic], I have to ask [pivot question]."

- "I'm thrilled to meet you; I've been wanting to connect and hear about what you are seeing in [hot topic or industry trend]."

- "Before I forget, I wanted to ask you a question about _____."

These can play out over email, in video calls, or in person. Taking a conversation and moving it toward (and into) the business discussion you want to have is not nearly as complicated as it feels.

Building a Business Conversation Doesn't Have to Feel Clunky

One more lesson on "owning the merge": it's important to smooth out transitions and recognize that conversations don't move in a straight line. Small talk is naturally sprinkled throughout a conversation and shows up throughout the trajectory of a relationship. Some of this requires practice, and some requires adapting an approach for a given client situation; the goal is to make sure it doesn't feel like too much too soon, or, conversely, seem that you're slow or uninterested. Also, realize that what you might think is a big ask is often not as big a deal to the client, and waiting too long to "own the merge" might mean you miss the opportunity. At some point, the client will hire counsel and that's going to be whoever invested in the relationship. If you aren't making the ask and guiding the conversation, someone else is.

When you're exiting a parking garage into traffic, waiting timidly at the side of the road hoping someone will let you in isn't effective. The analogy holds when it comes to getting a client's attention, too. They're busy juggling priorities. They have a life to manage, just like you do. They're not aware that you're standing shyly in the wings, hoping they notice you. Take the chance to inch into the conversation with small talk, just like you would use your blinker to signal that you're ready for the merge. But then, if you don't start to move forward, you're likely to stay at the edge, hoping something will happen. Instead, take control of the conversation and the next steps and then own the merge. Have the confidence to move forward and the belief that you belong in the conversation. Everything else is logistics.

The fact is that your chances of getting what you want if you don't try are effectively nil. Spot an opening and find the courage to pull into it, and you'll be in a much better place compared to waiting for the parking lot to empty. Trust me: showing up and being present changes your position from hoping the conversation will happen to being the organizer and leading right from the start. For right now, I want you to practice showing up, saying *Hello*, and then asking your clients, colleagues, or friends to *Tell You More*.

Be Predictable
in Your Approach

*Building trust starts by
staying consistent in the way
you show up for your clients.*

My husband loves to browse department stores to explore
the options before committing to buying anything. For me,
though, the sensory overload of it all is too much. Nothing
drives this home more than the olfactory assault of the perfume counters, each offering a sample or a spray, trying to
get the product in front of you. It makes me feel like I need
to run through the gauntlet of scents to get to the other side,
where I can finally pause, breathe, and look around.

When you consider the barrage of notes from attorneys and
advisors shamelessly touting their own expertise to their
clients (and potential clients), it can seem a lot like one of
those perfume tunnels. It's no wonder clients often seem to
race past these advisors, worried they might get caught in
a conversation.

When you set out to share what makes you great at what
you do to try to attract clients who need your knowledge
and skills, you need to consider how you're sending out that

message. On the one hand, there is an impulse to pair the message with a billable hour. After all, as a professional service provider, your expertise has value. On the other hand, many firms pump out a great deal of freely available thought leadership online to highlight their deep bench of attorneys.

Clients often look to these touchpoints to understand your expertise and approach. They also want to know what to expect regarding how you will share the important knowledge they want and need. When you are consistent in your approach, you set these expectations for your client and your team advances the relationship. In this area, consistency means having a reliable, predictable, repeatable approach.

Most of this chapter will address how you can share your expertise in a way that builds on the trust you have already created. Using your knowledge from the conversation you've been having enhances your thought leadership and work product. The goal? Engage more clients and referrals as you build trust by clearly understanding them and being the expert they need on their side.

A Social Strategy

There are many channels for communicating your messages. A blog, newsletter, podcast, or webinar are all great platforms for reminding clients of your expertise and getting in front of breaking updates that could affect their priorities and decisions. Social media platforms have created a modern-day stage from which to share your expertise. As discussed when we curated your Nurture List, as of this writing, LinkedIn is widely considered the best social platform for professional networking and the most widely used to share thought leadership posts, articles, and updates.

The thing to keep in mind is that no matter which or how many platforms you use, the way you present yourself needs to be consistent. When your tone and approach are aligned across all the places you show up, you signal that you are predictable and reliable and reinforce the trust the client will have in knowing how you will show up for the more tense, important moments in an advisory relationship. While everything else feels like it's changing quickly and constantly, your ability to convey your expertise in a consistent way keeps your client relationships strong and provides a constant stream of information you can share and use as part of your advice and counsel with Ideals.

Social media is also a great way to implement an amplification strategy that allows you to showcase how your work resonates with clients, encourages others to feel comfortable with you and your approach, and acts as a natural relationship expander. My suggestion is to start with a simple amplification strategy that aligns with you, your practice, and your clients.[26]

Sharing Content is a Journey, not a Destination

I created my LinkedIn account in 2007 when the platform was just four years old. LinkedIn's big claim at the time was that it was a central location to post your resume and make it easy for people to find you. For the next 12 years, other

---

26 If you're struggling to land on an approach to social media that feels right for you, a great place to start is with the #BizDeb Amplification Analyzer. Through a series of quick questions, it will provide you with a practical and effective recommendation for using social media to support your business goals. You can find it at https://debfeder.com/ampalign.

than an occasional scroll or adding a bit of information to my profile, that was how I used LinkedIn. Even when I launched my own business, I had no interest in exploring the platform further.

Up to that point, my business-generation strategy was based on referrals and simple conversations, and it had been extremely effective. Even so, my coach at the time kept trying to help me see the growth and opportunities that might await me on LinkedIn. At one point, she dared me to post something and see what happened. I don't shy away from that kind of throwdown, and with a few hours to spare ahead of the deadline she'd set for me, I posted my story. Smugly, I asked, "What now?" She simply smiled. Forty-eight hours later, I had landed a new firm client, seemingly out of the blue. When I asked them who had passed my name to them, they told me that they'd seen my post on LinkedIn. While that moment will stay with me forever, it's even better when it happens for my clients.

This was the greatest reality check I could have received. The platform I'd been avoiding had just delivered for me. But I also realized something else: it could deliver for my clients as well. Whether or not you want to be on platforms like LinkedIn, you need to acknowledge that your clients, colleagues, and connections use them. They want to look you up, see what you've been up to, and figure out whether they want to take that call from you.

Given that, using social media—whether it's your profile, your picture, or more in-depth content—to convey a consistent brand for your expertise is the next step in building trust with your clients and prospective clients.

Content Creation is Simply a Different Type of Conversation

New clients often tell me they've been trying to get Linke-dIn to work for them but that nothing has converted yet. This is usually because they've limited their activity to lurking around the platform, scrolling through messages, and posting ad-hoc on random topics, hoping this will garner some attention.

However, platforms like LinkedIn work best when you apply your understanding of your Ideal to drive content that connects with them. When done authentically and purposefully, this allows you to show up consistently and predictably and become known—all trust builders.

Use what you learned from getting curious to amplify your expertise and connect to more people (in your existing network and when adding new connections) to drive more conversations. Magic happens when you apply your learning, validate your expertise and perspective from conversations with clients, and frame it to resonate for your audience. Again, this calls for a blend of skills.

Content Strategy Made Simple

If you don't align online activity with your conversation strategy, your LinkedIn efforts will be like shouting into the wind. They will work about as well as standing in the corner at a noisy networking event, giving a speech, and hoping others come over, listen, be impressed, and decide to do business with you. It's not going to happen.

Conversely, using what you learn in client conversations (not the private, confidential stuff, of course) to create and post content you think is important and interesting to clients, will signal that you are paying attention, and that you get them.

What are the ingredients for creating content that resonates? The recipe includes:

- Topics you're discussing with your clients, competitors, and colleagues, as well as other topics you're interested in talking about that are relevant to your field

- The tone and tenor your clients relate to and expect from you

- Insights, informed by your expertise and experience, framed in a way that's professionally appropriate and client-generating (not reputation-destroying)

- Posts that make people pause and want to learn more

The goal is to create and sustain discussions that energize you, use what you learn, and link back to the conversations you're having with your clients. Content that works reminds people they need to call you, speak with you, and get your perspective on an issue. It also serves as the sticky stuff that keeps relationships together.

How do you know what type of LinkedIn content will work for you? Test content and tweak it by analyzing the engagement it gets and the conversations it generates so you can better guide your efforts and support your larger practice goals.

Activity

Pick one topic that is a focus of conversations in your practice area. If you need ideas, check conference agendas for the titles of breakout sessions. Industry publications often have great ideas hidden in the most recent articles as well.

Once you pick a topic, make three lists:

1. What myths about this topic would you like to refute?

2. What questions do clients always ask about this topic?

3. What is the background, history, or bigger context around this topic that needs to be understood and considered?

Each point on each of these lists is a sub-topic and could be its own social media post. Start with one sub-topic that brings you the most energy and excitement, and draft your post. Keeping your post focused on just one sub-topic will make it more approachable than if you make it more complex and try to cover everything all at once.

Now that you have some ideas to post about, it's time to find the best way to amplify it. I've found that the best social media content feels like great small talk at a cocktail party. In fact, LinkedIn itself is like a big party, with lots of animated conversations happening at once. You want to engage in small group conversations that resonate for you and your clients and start additional discussions that do the same for others.

I have four guidelines for amplifying your ideas online:

1. Be careful using LinkedIn to drive an argument. When it is a social issue of the utmost importance, that is one thing. But when it is content that is focused on your practice or the work of your clients or colleagues, pause and consider what conversations might come out of it. Often, less is more.

2. Language matters as much online as it does in a conversation. Choose words that are approachable and appropriate, and apply the same rules that you would in a conversation. Avoid posting inflammatory posts and language, as this will create unnecessary barriers between your work and your Ideals. You want to be sure no one is making inaccurate assumptions about you and your work before they even meet you.

3. Use your content to connect people to the real you; that is the cornerstone of a strong social media strategy (and a good rule of thumb for your entire client relationship strategy). In fact, when potential clients first talk with me, they often say they feel like they already know me from my content.

4. Think ahead about the conversations you engage in and be careful of walking into (or starting) conversations that will deter clients or run counter to positions you want to take in the future.

Now that you understand the guidelines, there are three rules to follow as you start creating content for LinkedIn (or any other platform):

Rule #1: Stay Current, but with a Twist

Rather than simply following the crowd and posting the same pop culture everyone else is talking about, use the platform as a launching pad for something unique and on brand. Think more deeply about the story to find sub-themes or sub-questions, ones that can expand the conversation and get you into the discussion authentically.

Example: AI—how to use it, when to use it, and what it's useful for—is a particularly hot topic right now. Regardless of your practice, an easy way to create conversation online around this theme would be with something like:

> *If I asked AI to explain [insert your practice area], it would share something like [add something broad and not quite on point about your practice area], yet it would forget to mention [pick one thing to share about your practice area that is part of a bigger discussion].*

This uses a current, trending topic as a launching pad for a deeper, relevant discussion about your practice and approach.

Rule #2: Article Sharing

While sharing articles and updates of interest can be a great way to extend the reach of your work, simply posting online without any further context is like walking into someone's home, throwing a magazine down on their coffee table, and walking out. You wouldn't do that. The analogous reaction on LinkedIn would be crickets, as everyone quietly scrolls past the post without engaging. Why? You haven't given them a reason to read the article. Instead, extract a small quote (or theme) from the article and expand on it in your post, linking through to the full article for more context.

Example: The bar journal has a great article about how senior associates can build a book of business. You might send the article to a colleague to ask if they'd add any tips to the list or how they might incorporate the article ideas for generating business. Both strategies expand the conversation. I recently contributed to such an article and often use it as a discussion prompt to see what else we need to add to the list (see how this simple strategy expands the opportunities to keep the conversation going?).[27] One caution: please don't share articles in a way that makes it feel like a sales pitch. Your goal should be an approachable post that expands the conversation, not one that feels like that perfume-counter gauntlet walk.

Rule #3: Keep Your Content a Low Lift

When content is too complex or dense, it can get lost on the audience. There's no need to dumb it down, but keep your content at an approachable level. That will allow your Ideals to recognize your experience for what it is and bring you into the conversation without feeling like you're talking over their heads.

Example: When a new statute provides ten new criteria to consider, you could share all ten in a quick list or break them down one at a time. This approach allows the reader and your clients to understand your expertise quickly. Even without reading through detailed reports or updates, they'll get that you are smart, knowledgeable, and the one to talk to about how to implement these criteria.

---

27 Kevin Penton's article, "How Senior Associates Can Build Their Books of Business," is a great resource (and was a fun interview). You can find the article here: https://www.law360.com/pulse/articles/1817998

The goal of posting content is to have people reach out to you to expand the conversation, bring you an issue that aligns with your expertise, or refer you as the one to know precisely because you are right in the mix and engaging in these conversations. You're setting the stage for the next conversation from the content you post.

Just Start

Many clients have used the simple strategy you just learned to engage their audience on LinkedIn and have experienced these results:

- Former clients reach out and want to learn more

- Colleagues and clients reach out and let them know the content was helpful and that they didn't realize this was the sort of work they do

- New clients reach out because they happened upon the post and are in this space themselves

Activity

If you're hesitant to start your own LinkedIn journey by posting content and commenting on other people's posts, there is an excellent first step. Take ten minutes and scroll through LinkedIn. Check out what your clients, their companies, and your competitors are posting about. When you find a post that grabs your attention, add your own comment to it.

Finding your own unique social media approach will encourage others to engage with you and give clients and colleagues permission to participate in your conversation.

When LinkedIn Isn't for You

As I mentioned earlier, while LinkedIn is a great platform to amplify your message and test out your own approach, there are plenty of other platforms where you can do this as well. YouTube is great for sharing video content, while Medium is a platform that caters to longer-form articles. Firm alerts and client updates are fantastic internal publications and a sort of platform in their own right that can be shared with a wider audience. You might take content from one platform and expand it to become a keynote speech or a webinar to further expand your expertise and professional platform.

No matter the platforms you choose, be sure they are aligned with where your clients congregate and where your Ideals are seeking advice and counsel. At the end of the day, your goal is to be considered the one to know because you are the expert in the room, and these platforms are excellent assets to help you accomplish that goal.

Part Three

**Everyday Choices
for a Thriving Thinking
Partner Practice**

Be the Expert in the Room

Your clients want to work with someone who knows their stuff and is willing to share it.

When I first started practicing law, there was a partner at my firm who was a finance guru. He could structure the most complicated of deals and break them down for anyone to understand. On Fridays, we would all meet for happy hour, and he would hold court as everyone brought him their big deal-structure questions to solve, often using tabletop peanuts and candy to illustrate how a deal was formed. When you can break down something incredibly complicated by sorting the M&Ms on the table, you're not only considered smart, you're known as the expert.

Everyone wants to demonstrate their expertise in conversations with clients and connections; that's natural. The key is to be strategic in how you do it and allow your expertise to land in a way that allows others not only to recognize it, but also respect it and want to know more about you and the work you do. It is one of the fundamental pillars of being a trusted thinking partner.

Let's discover how your expertise can shine through ... without you looking like a show-off.

When Given the Choice, Be the Expert

There is a fine line between touting your expertise and confidently presenting yourself as the expert. The former comes from a place of insecurity and often looks like a race to be the smartest and loudest in the room. It's reminiscent of those kids who always had to have the last word in class discussions. It's more effective to share your expertise in such a way that clients recognize your confidence and your willingness to engage productively and collaboratively on topics with anyone (even competitors). There is always someone out there who knows more about a topic, so engaging in a race of knowledge is often fruitless.

Trying to sound smart by deploying obscure vocabulary and asking big, complex questions doesn't usually come from confidence in your expertise but from insecurity. You do need to be knowledgeable, but knowledge isn't very helpful if you can't explain it, share it, or make it digestible and applicable to your colleagues and clients. When you can do these things, people not only recognize that you're intelligent, but they also see you're confident in your expertise.

Authentic Expertise Shines Through

We live in a rapidly changing world, especially where expertise is concerned. Clients can ask ChatGPT for the background on an issue or to break it down and simplify it for them. What they need your expertise for, then, is to know the right questions to ask, where to find the complete answer, and to help them consider what opportunities and obstacles may emerge from the decisions made today. It is that blend of judgment, experience, and knowledge that AI can't give them. This distinction is what sets a thinking partner apart from the crowd (or the bot). This is the person you want to be.

Just Keep Learning

There really aren't any shortcuts to being seen as "the expert." Instead, you need to dive into your area, keep learning about it, and be confident engaging in conversations about topics that let you expand your knowledge. There will be some areas where you won't have the answer at your fingertips, but you always want to be able to find the information so you can be accurate in your analysis. This means staying on top of your learning game, especially as you home in on your niche. Some ways to do this include:

1. **Block time each week to catch up on journals, articles, and updates in your field**. This will help you to think critically about who it might help and how and give you a sense of what's coming down the pike. Do you notice how this is learning and sharing all at the same time?

2. **Search LinkedIn**. If there's a hot topic trending, someone is already talking about it. Learn how others are discussing the subject so you can identify where your perspective might differ from that of the crowd. When you share both points of view and articulate the difference between them, that can be a green flag for a client to say, "We found the expert!"

3. **Set up a web alert that sends relevant information right to your inbox**. It might take a bit of work to get the search correct, but once you do, it will automate a good deal of what previously could suck up a lot of time. Let the tools and resources you have work for you. With all the information we now have to sift through, this can be an efficient way to stay on top of your expertise. Alerts keep you in the loop with what other experts are talking about; that's important because you can't assume you always know the full story.

Those who have made it to the partnership level and built a book of business understand that you grow a practice and expand that book by working with people who are the experts in their fields, who your clients want and need on their teams. Your clients need a deep bench of expertise, and offering this full package where others are invested in their practices, like you, will be a game changer for how you can approach business development and client relationships. Make sure your teams (and firm) believe in delivering excellence by learning and growing, and you'll have found yourself an important differentiator.

Getting the Word Out About Your Expertise

Sharing your expertise is a combination of marketing, business development, and client relationship strategies. While there are many ways to be known as the expert, one particularly effective strategy is to create content that keeps your clients and colleagues informed on hot topics and share it through expert discussions in public forums that break down complicated issues and analyze current trends. This doesn't mean that you have to be a full-time content creator. Rather, you simply need to find the kind of forum that works for your practice and where your clients show up for answers. In this age of Google, you never know who might find you through online content searches. I know of clients finding their attorneys after reading about their expertise in articles that are more than a decade old.

Here are a few suggestions to amplify your expertise using this strategy:

- Love what you do and feed that interest by studying the issues, trends, and topics related to it. For some, this will be substantive; for others, it will be procedural. Most often, it's a blend that works best for your personal approach.

- Subscribe to publications that cover industry and topical trends, and take note of who the most frequent and reliable contributors are. Avoid (or unsubscribe from) the less reliable ones.

- When you're asked to write, speak, or moderate a discussion, say yes. Test which publications, events, and other forums are most impactful for you to build your profile. (Hint: the publications from the previous point are a good place to start.)

- Get to know and befriend colleagues whom you consider competitors. Confident experts are often great friends with others in the same field. There is room for multiple voices in all areas, and getting to know others in your niche helps expand the conversation. You also benefit from seeing how others look at and process similar projects and from learning what differentiates you and your firm in the market.

- Be willing to share hot topics in a timely manner. When important news breaks, time is of the essence.

Sharing your expertise can start at any stage in your practice. Collaborating with others, researching hot topics, and staying up to date on trends allows you to not only learn the issues but also clarify your interests and focus as you develop your own professional brand.

Find Your Personal Practice Style

My client Matilda (whom I previously wrote about in *After Hello*) loves her work so much that she's often found reading case opinions and judicial analyses in her free time (yes, even the footnotes). When clients come to her with an issue, she's eager to fill them in on all the issues that come into play; she really knows her stuff. The cool thing about Matilda, though, is how she combines her love of the subject matter (and procedural issues) with her love of conversation. She has built her networking and business development goals around what she nerds out on all day, and that's magic. Her enthusiasm is contagious, which makes it exceedingly simple and straightforward for clients to engage with her. Matilda's practice style is crystal clear, and it resonates with the clients and colleagues she wants to work with. They appreciate her work and how much she loves the law, and they trust that she is (and will stay) on top of her game.

Be like Matilda. Know what you want your practice to look like, including where and how you want your expertise to shine. The magic, like Matilda's, is in sharing it authentically.

This might seem like a tall order in the middle of your busy practice and crazy-full life. But remember what you love about your practice. This can energize you to think about how you might combine that passion with your knowledge and confidently share it without feeling like you're wearing a sandwich board.

Choosing to amplify what makes you stand out in your field helps shape your professional brand and provides a great description of how you work, what you focus on, and how you help clients. When you can articulate this, your professional presence shines, and you build trust with those around you. Why? Because they know what to expect from you: you are predictable, consistent, and reliable. Put another way, a strong professional brand ensures that the right clients know you are the one who can be the advisor at their side during their most challenging moments (and biggest celebrations).

Activity

Professional branding is much easier when you put your expertise in the story. Think about what defines you, your practice, and what you bring to the foundational client relationships in your practice. Consider:

1. **How you practice**. What do you want people to say about what it's like working with you and how you manage projects?

2. **Your background**. What makes your path to this practice unique? What has informed and influenced your expertise?

3. **Your style**. Style refers not only to your clothing but also to the flair you bring to the practice. Are you the researcher? The meticulous detail tracker? The strategist? The closer? Claim a title and own it. I know mine, but I don't want to influence yours, so I won't share it just yet.[28]

Think about the attributes you uncovered through this brainstorm. Be sure you aren't just choosing words you think are important because everyone else uses them. Your practice personality needs to be authentically yours.

You build a trusted thinking partnership when you have the skills and knowledge to be useful and the confidence to let it shine. In previous chapters, the focus was on connecting at a human level. Now, you are using your knowledge and experience to make your relationships stronger. This starts with using your expertise to break down complicated issues for clients and help them make good decisions. Your experience helps you find your own way of connecting with your audience and allows your practice personality to shine. Always aim to gather your Ideals around the table and explain complicated topics in a way that makes them want to grab a bag of popcorn and nerd out right along with you.

---

28 If you send me an email telling me about your personal practice style and approach, I will share mine with you too. Send a note to hello@debfeder.com.

Be There

Never underestimate the long-lasting impact of showing up and caring.

Winters in the Midwest are no joke, and January of 2024 arrived with a barrage of snow days, blizzard warnings, sub-zero temperatures, and icy conditions that made even the most experienced drivers extra cautious. Yet life continues. So, parents scrambled to advise their kids on how to navigate the conditions to get back on the road and back to school or work.

In one example, my dear friend Mary called me and asked for advice for driving between Kansas City and Iowa. She cared nothing for my hard-won knowledge of the best food stops. Instead, she wanted to know the best day for her son to drive back to school. I put out a few quick texts to friends in Iowa, and then Mary and I got on a call and walked through the scenarios. Mostly, I just listened.

Once Mary got her son on the road, she called back to share how they processed the decision and to reflect on our chat. What Mary appreciated was not any huge insight I'd shared but how, in the middle of her need, I had her scooch over and sat next to her on the (virtual) bench and simply stayed there through the process.

I love this image because it conveys what a trusted thinking partner does when supporting a client who is processing a big decision. When they call their advisor, the client often already has a sense of the advice they need. Yet, talking through the background and any internal politics at play starts to shape a more complete picture for the attorney. Getting the client to *Tell You More* opens up options and allows you to give better advice. This is a best practice to help others manage and process complicated decisions. This is the role of the thinking partner.

Knowing when and how to navigate moments that help you grow into this role is about pacing (smothering doesn't work) and presence (being calm and open rather than hurried and harassed).

Being the trusted thinking partner is not always for a defined billable project. Moving a client from hiring you for one or two projects to leaning on you for daily decisions means showing up consistently to help them process their issues with your expert advice and then sometimes sitting by their side while they worry and wait.

This may be waiting for a jury verdict or a shareholder vote or deciding whether to pursue the merger or take a proposal to the board of directors. For clients, these moments can feel like driving on a snow-covered highway and trying to avoid patches of ice. When you're the advisor who shows up, sits next to them on the bench, and stays with them for as long as it takes, you create the opportunity for connection and a business relationship without ever making a slick formal pitch.

Drop the Harried Act

When you're eyeballs deep in work, and someone asks, "How are you?" you may be tempted to answer with something along the lines of:

- "So busy I can't see straight."
- "Exhausted."
- "Too much to do, but getting it done."
- "Swamped."

If it's a client you're responding to, these responses send the signal that you're too busy to spend more than a quick moment with them on their pressing matters. While this might be true, it can leave clients feeling that you can't handle their next project, let alone provide them with timely, everyday advice.[29] Moving from being a lawyer working on a project to the role of a trusted thinking partner starts with your ability to be present whenever your client needs you most.

---

29 This is not to diminish or dismiss the very real exhaustion that comes with a busy practice and layers of competing priorities. There *is* a way to discuss this very important topic, find balance and boundaries, and open a dialogue that doesn't block it the way the language of exhaustion does.

Activity

This exercise is designed to help you notice the language of exhaustion:

1. List the ways you see or hear others express signs of being exhausted, fed up, or too busy.

2. What words or phrases make you feel someone is not interested in working with you?

3. Are there non-verbal cues that send the same signal?

4. Do you have a standard small-talk response that you lean on when someone asks how you're doing? Does it have a note of exhaustion or of being overworked in it?

5. How often do you refer to busyness or exhaustion when sharing updates with colleagues and clients?

Once you notice the language of exhaustion, you can decide how you want to change it or use it productively to open a different discussion.

Now that you recognize the language that can cut off opportunity, it's time to focus on creating a language of connection and, more importantly, a language of support and care. Sometimes, that "language" is non-verbal. For example, I provided support and care for Mary by allowing her to talk and by listening attentively. Knowing when to share and when to listen takes practice. The opportunities to expand a client relationship don't always come in high-pressure, action-packed moments but often show up when you stand in the wings as a supporting player.

Pace for Longevity

A successful legal practice needs to have a constant stream of projects and clients coming in the door. This requires you, as the professional advisor and thinking partner, to pace your relationship for the problems and legal work on the horizon. Often, neither of you will know about these things ahead of time. That's why it's important that you actively keep in touch with your clients and answer their emails, texts, and calls. Emergencies can come out of nowhere, and they can rarely wait for a lunch that you've penciled into the calendar for some time in the next four to six weeks. You'll be top of mind only when you've been consistently and reliably available all along.

Activity

Set a timer for three minutes to scroll through your inbox and make a list of the following contacts:

1. Who has reached out to you that you haven't had time to respond to?

2. Who do you need to check in on to see how their project or challenge is shaping up?

These connections may be looking to expand their work with you and waiting for you to seize the opportunity.

The Supporting Role is Often the Strongest

The conversation in a client relationship begins with *Hello* and expands by listening to what the client says, noticing what they aren't saying, and identifying the opportunities where you can act (do work for them) and those instances where you should just be present (give them the space to process their decisions) for high-stakes situations.

For lawyers in a labor and employment practice, advising clients is inextricably bound up with providing emotional support for those incredibly difficult decisions that directly impact people's livelihoods. One particularly stressful situation is when a client needs advice and support to implement layoffs at their business.

A client of mine named Jack, who works in labor and employment law, typically starts his conversation with such clients by saying, "I am the lawyer you don't want to be calling." Clients who call him for layoff support come into the relationship fully conscious of the fact that things aren't going well (neither for their individual company nor for their industry as a whole) and that the impact of their decisions goes well beyond their personal welfare. For this reason, a critical component of Jack's business development strategy is being a safe sounding board while advising on the technical requirements of the situation. Being efficient and effective opens the door, but being responsive and available as clients make these intense decisions moves him into the role of trusted thinking partner. That is the role you want to be in as your practice grows.

Learning More

Preparing for a client meeting often starts with a quick Google search and LinkedIn scan, followed by an internal search for who is connected to the client and knows their priorities and plans.

After research and preparation, things then happen in real time as the client conversation begins. Listening and knowing how and when to interject with your own stories and insights helps advance the relationship. Understanding the client's worries and fears and checking in on them demonstrates your care.

Present for the Emotional and Complicated Decisions

When you are working with clients at the top of their field or who are working in fast-paced, growing markets, you're working with people who face complicated questions every day. As they weigh their choices and decide on next steps, they need someone to support them. This is frequently the role of the trusted legal advisor. Confidentiality supports this relationship, and expertise backs it up. With a view of the broader landscape their clients are dealing with and the pitfalls they may encounter, the legal advisor also provides emotional support for clients who may be experiencing nervousness.

Nerves can look different in a professional context than they do in a personal one. A nervous mother might wring her hands or tear up. A nervous business leader can have big emotions too, but these are more likely to show up as micromanaging, anger, or aggressive behavior, for example. While you need to make sure your technical work is good and your advice is solid, managing the client's emotions requires you to stay calm. But how do you offer this type of support, which the client may not ask for explicitly?

The easiest way to gain permission to support clients this way as a trusted thinking partner to lean on is to ask for it. The best approach and the right question to ask depends on the situation. Here are some common scenarios:

1. The client tries to process their situation by throwing every option (as well as the kitchen sink) at you as they share their problem. Your job here is to help them narrow down the choices and the details they need to decide.

    The question: "What further information would help you process these choices?"

    What it provides: This asks clients to be more specific about what they want and need and is especially useful when it seems the details haven't yet been fleshed out.

2. The client comes to you for support when it seems clear to you that they don't have the right team at the table. The truth is, often, the client doesn't realize what they don't know because they don't have access to the right experts.

    The question: "How might pulling in additional experts better support you and your goals?" You might also simply offer to introduce them to colleagues who work in a similar space or have helpful advice that could be valuable to them.

What it provides: This expands the work you are doing with a client and brings in the whole team to better support them.

3. A frantic client who needs an anchor in the decision-making process asks you to pull together realistic options.

   The question: "What are the options that you can realistically envision right now? Are there any others you think should be considered?"

   What it provides: The discussion that needs to happen.

Having the ability to discern when the client needs you to solve the problem or simply to be a sounding board is the back-end work required of a thinking partner. All these conversations are worthy of your presence and care and each can be a game changer for building your practice and those incredible client relationships along the way.

Celebrate
Together

*Happy dances, cartwheels, and
high fives go a long way toward
building trust with your clients.*

The first time I was invited to a client's celebratory dinner, it was not for *closing* a deal but for showing up and leading a diligence team through a complicated search for information on a transaction that was just kicking off. Having been sent on the trip at the last minute, I'd not yet met the client and wasn't exactly prepared for the dinner. I remember rushing to a shopping mall asking a sales associate about the restaurant, and scrambled to find something to wear. This was before you could look up anyone and everything on social media, giving me no option but to just show up and meet the clients at dinner.

I appreciated the invitation to participate and spent the dinner getting acquainted with clients who, up to that point, had been in meetings with people who were far more important to the issue than I was. Getting to know them at that dinner led to closing the deal months down the road, which led to an even better celebratory dinner. Showing up and being there to celebrate the milestone with the clients paid dividends throughout that deal. I remember sitting in the steakhouse with that small group of clients, wondering how to get invited to the next big meeting with them and have the chance to join the next conversation (and lead that next team).

I didn't know it at the time, but being at that dinner and toasting their success was a huge trust-builder. My role that night was to congratulate them and show that I was authentically engaged with them as they moved to the next step. Beyond that, I showed that I could hold my own in the small talk and handle all the questions about the work I'd been leading, and I knew how we planned to tackle what was next.

Picking up the phone to check in, expanding conversations that started at a networking event, and being available to bounce ideas around with a client all build trust before the work begins. Being actively and enthusiastically involved in the conversations that happen *after* the work is done is something that clients notice and appreciate, too.

Said in terms my mother would approve of: thanking someone for inviting you is not only polite but also remembered. Following up a few weeks later to see how everything is progressing solidifies the relationship. Staying engaged after the work is complete builds a firmer foundation for what comes next in the client relationship. When you do this, the end of one project can be the beginning of the next stage in the client relationship.

Start with You

When was the last time you reflected on everything you accomplished in a week? We all spend a significant amount of time and energy paying attention to what still needs to get done: the next step in a project, the agenda for the upcoming meeting, managing the closing checklist—you get the picture. Yet even once these tasks are completed, the accomplishment typically goes by without fanfare. However, these small, everyday wins should be noted because they are often a reflection of progress with your client's project and how close you both are to crossing the finish line.

Celebration doesn't have to mean a big, all-hands-on-deck dinner. It can be as simple as a short congratulatory note that moves the project along.

What might this look like? Here's an example:

> You prepared for and attended negotiations for XYZ transaction. At the meeting, everyone agreed on the terms, and you sent them out for review.
>
> **Your accomplishment**: Preparing the agenda and leading the negotiation.
>
> **Your client's accomplishment**: Getting everyone to agree to the terms and the review in process.
>
> **The celebration**: "[Name of client], congratulations on getting everyone to come together and agree on the terms. I have sent out the terms, and as soon as we hear back, we can get rolling on documenting the deal. You were amazing in the meeting. Thank you for supporting the plan to use a term sheet moving forward."

Activity

Now it's your turn.

1. Make a list of everything you accomplished this week. Start by looking at your calendar for clues.

2. Next, grab your task list and recognize each milestone you hit and where you're at with each project. If the stage has changed, make sure to note it on the list before moving on.

3. Now, consider which of these items will be mirrored on your clients' lists.

4. Before you close your list, use a star to note which accomplishments are worthy of highlighting to the client.

5. Circle the ones that warrant a follow-up conversation and cross off ones that are completed or that you no longer need to focus on.

Create this list and complete this exercise every week.

Now that you have that weekly list, you can use it to support a client update, as the purpose for a call, and as a map to guide the work forward. The trust that is built by paying attention to these details (while also congratulating the client on your mutual progress) is one more valuable deposit in the trust bank.

An example of this strategy in action comes from my client, Laura. Laura is the consummate trusted thinking partner, which means that she is called on to support her clients when she least expects it. She often receives calls from clients at odd hours asking her business and legal questions about a project without any notice. This keeps her in the loop as an important part of the team. As her clients' projects progress, Laura picks up the phone (or texts, depending on the client's preferences) and sends a quick and simple congratulatory message. She also makes sure to pay attention to updates on LinkedIn and loves spotlighting her clients' new project announcements. Laura sees her clients' wins as her wins. In fact, she is excited for them whether or not she or her team were involved in the project. Dedicated to the relationship, she stays connected during every stage of her client's success.

A Collective Deep Breath

You know that moment when you finish a really great book, and the story comes to a satisfying conclusion, but you still want to know what happens next? When you follow up with a client after a project finishes, that's the sort of opportunity you have. It's like getting exclusive access to a sequel. The first of these opportunities happens soon after the closing. It's a chance to take a collective deep breath with the client and tidy up any outstanding threads. This conversation involves:

1. **Getting the client's perspective on how everything turned out**. Ask what they thought of the final outcome of the project. Keep the conversation simple, and remember to listen and learn.

2. **Saying thanks**. Express gratitude for being able to participate in the transaction or case. Without this, the impression may be that you wanted to be involved just to collect another billable hour or origination

credits. When you actively express gratitude, your character shines through.

3. **Supporting what's next**. Most projects don't have a hard ending that wraps everything up perfectly with a bow. Instead, when papers are signed, or a decision is handed down, it usually yields a fresh list of next steps. Offering to help, or at least confirming that everyone is on the same page regarding responsibility for the open items, is yet another trust-builder.

In fact, all of these are trust builders, and each offers the opportunity to be involved in what happens next. This type of post-closing follow-up is easy to calendar and important to remember.

Celebrations Aren't Always Big

A simple status update with clients is another way to recognize milestones and stay connected with clients through projects that may have a lengthy timeline (or no timeline at all). These smaller touchpoints are often overlooked. When remembered, these everyday connections keep projects and relationships on track and continue the trust-building cycle.

A weekly touch-base call to a client to recap what has been accomplished and congratulate them on completed milestones allows you to stay organized, keeps your team communicating with the client, and recognizes the progress with and for them.

This often works best with a checklist (or simple spreadsheet) and a reminder on your calendar. These calls are a good time to get questions answered for the following week's priority too. In my experience, some clients want to collaborate on call format and project tracking, while others simply want you to take care of it. Either way, this is a great chance to touch base, check in, and celebrate the small milestones that happen in a week.[30]

When you celebrate with a client, you create more alignment with the client, update each other on things you may not be aware of, and maintain forward momentum. The truth is, there is always the opportunity for a client to replace one team with another that shows that it cares more. Showing up and staying engaged goes a long way toward keeping your client from looking around for another, more responsive team to work with. Authentic enthusiasm for your client, their work, and their successes make the work and effort involved so much more rewarding and significantly more fun.

---

30 The #BizDeb monthly calendar often includes these weekly reflections as a reminder to do this. Spend five minutes each week reflecting on the celebrations you and your clients had. Reach out and call them to debrief or send a quick note congratulating them on the win.

The Thinking Partner's Everyday Choices

The smallest choices make the biggest differences each and every day.

Choosing to build a career with space for trusted thinking partners and allowing yourself to be one requires a commitment to show up and engage every day. Throughout this book, you've found suggestions for simple actions you can put in motion now without having to rethink your entire career. The best thing about building a practice filled with clients who trust you is that the more you focus on that, the faster your book of business grows. There is a compounding effect of trust and how others value your approach, expertise, and willingness to be the thinking partner at their side.

Using these ideas is an everyday choice. What could happen for you, your career, and these amazing relationships if you focus on deepening your trusted relationships over the next year? When you use these strategies, they layer to let you engage in better conversations, expand your network, and support your clients at a higher and deeper level. All of that increases the trust between you and your clients.

You have committed to building a practice by being intentional about bringing in clients. The options to come in this chapter can cultivate your network, progress conversations, and turn relationships into clients. I invite you to try each of them over the next few weeks and circle back to them over the next several months. Notice how consistent interactions and engagement with your network advance small talk into talking about what's next.

Try each of these strategies and reflect on how they work for you, how they resonate with clients, and how they help you be the thinking partner you want to be.

Grow Your Network

As discussed, a legal practice must continually cultivate a pipeline of work. Building the habit of deploying the following strategies, which generate new connections for your Nurture List, is a great investment.

Ask for an intro

Your connections know people whom you want to know. How do you get to know them? Ask for an introduction. This may come up in conversation when talking about work or about your focus, when someone says, "Oh, I have a friend/ colleague/client who works in that space." Don't hold back and wonder whether to ask for an introduction; go for it.

> "Wow, I would love the chance to connect with them and learn more about this work. Would you be willing to introduce us?"

> "What a small world! If it would make sense, I would love for the three of us to find a time to connect for a conversation and see if a collaboration makes sense."

Keep the ask simple and low pressure so you can follow up on it later. Don't follow up the next day, but after a week or two, and see if they need anything from you to make the connection.

Connect with your community

Your potential clients aren't always obviously so. Contrary to our expectations, they may be people you spend time with outside the office, like members of your gym, parents of your kids' classmates, or your neighbors. You may even know that one of these connections might be a potential client but have avoided approaching for fear of spoiling the friendship over a possible work opportunity.

The tactic here is super simple. Reach out and ask if you can grab coffee one morning after school drop-off to talk more about their current clients and find the space to share what you do. Keep the conversation efficient and make it easy for you both to fit it into your packed days. When the conversation happens, you will be able to let out a big sigh of relief that you took one step past the "friend zone" and expanded the conversation.

Be expansive in your networking

Awesome relationships often lead to more awesome relationships. Your status as a trusted team member is enhanced by your ability and willingness to introduce others and act as a connector. To facilitate this, the best questions might sound something like:

- "Who else do I need to know?"
- "Who else do you want to meet?"
- "Are there connections or resources you are looking for?"
- "Who else should we include in this conversation?"

Notice that these questions are focused on both parties. This isn't about grabbing new connections and building a ginormous network but about deepening your relationships by broadening the conversation. You are no longer only talking about one specific project but about expanding the scope of the dialogue and relationship. Follow through and nurture those new connections in the way you are known for.

Use reconnections to nurture and grow the network

A reconnection is someone you used to know, have since lost touch with, and want to get to know again. These could be old clients or colleagues, a former neighbor, or a friendship that has been quiet for a while. Reconnecting and catching up is a simple strategy that allows you to build a new foundation, learn more about them, and, if possible, help them with goals using the resources you have at your disposal. It's important that you don't overstep by making an immediate ask or commitment of someone that you haven't spoken to in a while. Authentically show up and care about catching up, just like you would with a client.

Be the Center of the Relationship

Relationships are both one-to-one and multi-node, and it's wise to think beyond yourself when building relationships and bring others into the conversations with clients. The following strategies can support this.

Introduce your team

Using your team's expertise to expand the work for a client is a powerful move that allows you to look out for their interests, and lets them build a deeper relationship with you and your team. This requires that your team shows up for the client the way you want them to and collectively and holistically nurtures the relationship. How do you do this without simply showing up on the client's doorstep with an entourage behind you? By asking about other projects and resources the client might need, you can then suggest an introduction to others. For example:

> *I noticed the article about your team working on [insert topic]. We put out a client alert from my colleagues who are working in this space, and I wanted to make sure you saw our update. Please let me know if I can help with an introduction or if you need any additional resources for your work on [insert issue].*

Participate in (or plan) a reunion

I recently attended a law firm reunion with colleagues who all practiced together. It was a great space to catch up with old friends, meet their colleagues, and find out what everyone was working on. At the event, the conversation pivoted to the question of how to work this type of room.

A reunion can be with a friend group, classmates, work colleagues, or clients. You might consider organizing such an event, as being the one who brings everyone together is always appreciated. Whether organizer or participant, once there, the key is to mingle rather than stick with the people you're already comfortable talking to. Keep mingling until you have reconnected with at least two people you look forward to reaching out to in the next week.

Know your own team

If you're in a large office, or a network of offices, make sure you know people in other locations and practice areas. This deepens your ability to bring in work for the firm, even if it's not for your own practice. A simple goal is to know some-one in each of your organization's offices. Having a go-to person to reach out to and quickly find the resources you need across the firm makes you a valuable person to know and helpful to your clients. A simple email can work well:

> Hi [insert name],
>
> I am working on making sure I know more people in our offices and have heard your name mentioned by several other partners. I would love to find time to connect and learn more about you and your work. Please let me know some times that might work with your schedule over the next few weeks.
>
> Thanks!
> [Your name]

The following alternative can work well when there is a meeting or conference coming up:

> Hi [insert name],
>
> I just saw your name on the list of people attending _____. I will also be there and would appreciate it if you have time to sit down and share with me a bit more about your practice and clients. I believe we might have some synergies in our work and would love to find ways to collaborate.
>
> Please let me know what your schedule looks like to meet.
>
> Much thanks,
> [Your name]

Put Your Expertise into the Conversation

We talked in the earlier chapters about making sure you are known as the expert. Putting in all that hard work to speak, write, and share your knowledge can be leveraged to also share with clients, colleagues, and referral partners.

Share your big idea

Often, you may know your client has been working on a big project, and you just can't stop thinking about it. Maybe you scratched out some notes the other day with a list of things they should consider, and you keep hoping they'll call and want to talk about it. Instead of waiting, reach out. Share that you have been mulling over some of the strategies after they shared about the project in the last meeting, and you have a few ideas they might want to consider. Open up an invitation and be sure to reply promptly when they want to learn more.

Extend the invitation

You've worked hard to put together an outstanding webinar with a great panel of experts from the firm. There are likely certain clients you want to invite. Send a simple note to let them know you'd like to invite them personally. Even if they can't attend, it's still a "win," as you will have something to share and follow up with them after the event. Another way to go above and beyond is to offer to come by and share the presentation highlights with their team in a private meeting.

Go ahead and talk shop

What if you end up at lunch with a good friend who just happens to be in the general counsel's office or is leading a team that is ready to hire, and you know you and your team would be the perfect fit? But you don't want to be too obvious, appear to be taking advantage of the situation, or make the friendship awkward. You want them to trust you and your intentions. Instead of trying to pitch anyone, think of a good question you can use to "put a pin" in the discussion and let you pivot into a business conversation. Start your lunch or conversation off with customary greetings, and then allow yourself this one sentence: "I can't wait to catch up, but remind me that I have one work question I want to ask before we leave lunch."

That's it. You dropped a pin in the opportunity, giving yourself permission to circle back to it at the end and bring up work. When you do this, one of three things will happen:

- They will ask you to jump in right then (and go for it),
- One of you will remember at the end, or
- You will both forget.

Even if you forget, you can circle back to this conversation over the phone after lunch. It is a natural segue to allow your mutual business interests to expand the conversation and include the opportunity to work together. If you are still concerned about the impact it might have, address the awkwardness up front. Knowing this and stating it is, again, a trust-builder.

Spread the word

You worked hard on that article, and now it's getting lots of attention. You posted it on LinkedIn, and your firm is blasting it everywhere. You might assume your client has seen it, but better than assuming is to make sure and send it over to them directly. This is a simple expression that shows you care about the issues they face every day. It is a way of reminding them that you have their back. It doesn't have to come across as braggy, though. The key is to note how the article and research address an issue that relates to a conversation you had, or how the article addresses a topic you know they're working on based on their institutional priorities. Your email might say something like:

> Hi [insert name],
>
> I hope all is well. I wanted to send over this article we just distributed, focused on [the subject matter and why it matters to them]. Let me know if you want to jump on a quick call to discuss once you've had a chance to read it over. Shout out with questions.
>
> [Your name]

Share your smarts without strings

Caring about a client while not intruding on the relationships they have with other advisors exudes confidence. You aren't trying to step on anyone's toes, but you do want to highlight your own expertise and diligence. This is best done when you know there's a case that impacts your clients, a regulatory update that affects them or their industry, or other news of interest that makes sense to pass along. While being proactive might step on some toes, you don't want the client to miss out on the information. A way of messaging this might be:

Hi [insert name],

I know you have a team already working on [insert case/transaction], but this [article/case/update] came across my desk, and I wanted to make sure you see it. Please let me know if you need any more details right now; otherwise, let's find a time to talk soon.

[Your name]

This is a powerful, confident approach that doesn't offer anything but support. Be that advisor, and you are one step closer to securing and solidifying your spot at the table.

Timing Matters

We can get wrapped up in sharing content and networking that both lawyers and clients can wonder if things are moving too fast or too slow. Instead of worrying, talk about timing openly.

Pre-approve the pacing

One of the most common worries among people seeking to be a trusted advisor is that you're bothering the client. However, the goal of being a trusted advisor is to be the one who *gets* bothered, or at least gets called all the time for the client to bounce ideas and ask questions. Your hope is to be the one the client *chooses* to bother.

The fear of nagging someone is real. How can you make sure you're welcome in their inbox? Ask for permission upfront. The key is to not be too obvious about it and to give yourself a plan for follow-up as part of your conversation. Something like this works well:

Typically, I find that touching base in __ weeks/months [or possi-bly days, depending on your work] to make sure we are all aligned helps. Would that work for you?

You'll get one of two responses to this. They may agree and when you connect with them again, they'll be expecting it. Or they may offer up alternative timing. This is equally effective as it still gives you permission to reconnect. Your job, then, is to make sure the follow-up is on the calendar so you don't drop the call. If you commit to a plan, follow through.

Stop chasing

Relax into your confidence; it's more powerful than you can imagine. Chasing work reeks of desperation; instead, back off a bit. Stay busy with other things and get comfortable touching base with something meaningful in a few weeks. Allow some space in the conversation. Unless they've asked for you to "jump," it's okay to take a couple of deep breaths and wait.

What's next

When the case finally settles, or the transaction closes, everyone seems eager to slam the book on the project and move on to other things. Well, I want you to stay engaged for just a bit longer. Linger and find out what the client is focused on now and get exposed to the next project and potential opportunities.

Your plan is to ask the one question that continues the conversation after the current project: "Once you catch your breath, what's next?"

This question expands the conversation beyond the case or transaction that has just been completed. It opens up conversations around broader topics like personal goals and plans as well as the opportunity to learn more about the client team and wider organizational priorities. The goal is to see where you might provide value and get to know the full picture that this colleague or client has in their view. It's not about landing a piece of that work now but knowing about it and allowing the opportunity to unfold.

Be direct

Waiting for someone to realize that you want a particular piece of work is a low-odds game, and that's risky when you have business development goals sitting in front of you and numbers you're trying to hit. One very simple but effective way to advance work with potential clients and to get colleagues to include you in their work is to be direct and ask for it. There is a variety of methods to go about this, none of which require you to be aggressive or sales-y:

> "I would love to get involved the next time a project like [insert details] comes across your desk."

> "I would like the opportunity to discuss ways we can support your work going forward. What would be the most helpful next steps?"[31]

> "If it makes sense for you and your team's goals, we would love to support this work and share our team's expertise with you."

---

31 Note: In this option you say "we" because you are not trying to expand the work from just you; you're proposing to share your entire team's expertise with the other partners across your firm.

While these strategies often end up blending into one another, you can pace them in a way that works for you and for your clients. Notice that each is a blend of mindset, relationship-building, progressing the conversation, and sharing your expertise. And the goal of each is the same: be the trusted thinking partner no matter what stage the relationship is at while understanding that often, the very best client relationships are even more awesome than you could have imagined they would be after that first *Hello*.

One More Thought

On my first day of work after taking the bar exam, I was given a tour of an empty office with a calendar stuck to the wall. On it, one day was noted with a star. The young partner responsible for the tour made a point of stopping in the office and asking me if I had any idea what that calendar represented. I didn't have a clue, and so she explained. The attorney who worked in the office had decided that, on that starred day, everything on her plate would be done.

I often reflect on the irony of that calendar and that attorney's hope of getting everything done. Because the goal of a practice is to fill it with amazing clients and projects that do not end but grow.

There is certainly no fixed end date to building incredible, trusting relationships with your clients. There is no one day when the client sends you balloons and confetti with a note that says, "I finally trust you!" And you certainly don't want them to say, "No more." In fact, your goal is the exact opposite. Trust and the level of work they trust you to take on with them develops and deepens over time. As you invest time and energy in the client relationship, look around and reflect frequently on how you know trust exists and that there are opportunities to connect.

Earning and building trust is a process. It happens in both the small, everyday moments and the larger, long-term commitments; it is solidified in your consistency and reliability. It is, in essence, living up to your reputation.

The best relationships are those where both sides strive for excellence. Clients who want excellent representation know to invest in the advisors they need by their side. Lawyers who get this show up and engage in the conversations necessary to become and remain the sought-after thinking partner. This is not done on any one day—it's a road you walk together every day with your team of thinking partners.

The practice of law is a hard one. It often feels like a race to keep up with ever-changing industry, political, business, and statutory frameworks. The only certainty is that things change, and no two projects are ever really the same. Seeing and understanding the nuances in the issues is important and understanding the client—the person—on the other end of the phone is equally so.

Work and life go best when we have others by our side who get us and support the work we do. Believe this for yourself, as it makes the journey much more fun. The levity and enjoyment in this career come not only in big celebrations or retirement dinners but also in the everyday interactions you have with your colleagues and clients.

A trusted thinking partnership often looks like this:

- Sharing a good laugh and banter at the beginning of a call

- Seeing something on a store shelf that reminds you of a client and sending them a picture (and not thinking that's weird)

- Inviting clients to meet up for coffee, lunch, or a drink, and not worrying if they say yes or no

- Knowing the names of your clients' kids and them knowing yours

- Sharing about a hobby or travel plans, without concern about them stalking you at your location to bother you about minutiae

- Someone sitting by your side when life happens, and you need a safe space to cry, take a break, or walk away

- Asking someone to jump in and cover something, and knowing they've got it (and how to practice this in return)

Put simply, the trusted relationship feels solid. It feels honest in its approach, and it feels real in the care you have for the client, the work, and your dedication to sharing your expertise. It is about showing up when asked or when you know it's needed, and not worrying when you haven't heard back. It is an alignment of energy and priorities. When this all comes together, the work is fun, and the next opportunities are apparent. We started with *Hello*, asked others to *Tell You More*, and then navigated the everyday moments that create a solid practice. From this new vantage point, problems are solved, and opportunities are discovered from the trusted belief in our clients and colleagues. Know how to navigate the work this brings in and the options that come next, and you'll realize that there is always plenty to go around.

Acknowledgments

Once again, I am at a loss for words for how to thank all those who have invested their personal time, energy, and input into *Tell Me More*. I must start with the two best thinking partners around: my siblings. Michael and Julia, your willingness to take every call, bounce ideas, read drafts, and tell me when I'm off base is deeply appreciated. To my kids, Izzi and Elliott, your patience is noticed, and I'm especially grateful for your strong input when my ideas go a little too far. Andrew, your openness to be part of the story and up for any conversation is how it all began.

Beyond my family, my gratitude extends to my clients. For each of you who shared a story, anecdote, challenge, or win, you enrich the work I do every day. For those willing to show up to laugh, sing, and dance together, your courage and commitment are truly valued. Being part of your professional story is an honor, each and every day.

To my team, starting with my two coaches, Ryan and Matt, there's not enough gratitude for reminding me that I'm stronger than I think and for helping me strive for excellence.

To all those that helped bring the words to the page, thank you. Jeff and Shelly, I'm grateful for the pages of notes from that initial outlining session through the final draft. Lisa, you made walking through the weeds of this book a ton of fun. The Evolution Audio team, your attention to detail is unmatched and you make sound recording something to look forward to. Brian Gayley, your photography makes any cover look incredible.

To the Smith Publicity team, you truly are the gold standard of excellence, and I'm honored to have you helping me share my work with the world. To Scott, Carolyn, Ania—and the entire Grammar Factory Publishing team, I knew we were a great fit from the first conversation and the meticulous timeline you presented. I appreciate all of your incredible insight, patience, and commitment to *Tell Me More*.

Finally, to my dad, Ron, for always bringing us to client dinners and cocktail parties. You showed by example what it means to build trusted thinking partnerships with incredible clients, and to accept nothing less.

About the Author

Deb Feder is a business development and practice management strategist and coach for lawyers and law firms. Her work focuses on helping lawyers and professionals attract consistent clients through curious, confident conversations. For the past decade, Deb has been committed to reimagining work-life balance, building healthy careers, and tackling high-stakes work, enabling big careers while preserving personal time.

Prior to founding Feder Development, Deb practiced corporate law for 15 years. She holds a history degree from the University of Michigan and a JD/MBA from the University of Iowa. Deb is the author of *After Hello: How to Build a Book of Business, One Conversation at a Time*, a guide to building a thriving law practice based on a blend of mindset, strategy, and practical solutions. She also contributed to *#Networked: How 20 Women Lawyers Overcame the Confines of COVID-19 Social Distancing to Create Connections, Cultivate Community & Build Businesses in the Midst of a Global Pandemic*.

Known for her interactive and engaging approach, Deb facilitates retreats and workshops on business development, productivity, client relationships, authenticity, and communication. She resides in Kansas City with her family.